I BELIEVE
IN ONE GOD

BENEDICT XVI

I Believe
in One God

The Creed explained

with a Foreword by
Archbishop Vincent Nichols

ST PAULS

Cover design: DX Imaging

© 2012 Libreria Editrice Vaticana
00 120 Citta del Vaticano
www.libreriaeditricevaticana.com

© 2012 Edizioni San Paolo s.r.l.
Piazza Soncino, 5 - 20092 Cinisello Balsamo (Milano)
www.edizionisanpaolo.it

© 2012 ST PAULS-UK
ST PAULS Publishing
187 Battersea Bridge Road, London SW11 3AS, UK
www.stpaulspublishing.com

Back cover photograph © copyright Periodici San Paolo s.r.l.

ISBN: 978-0-85439-840-9

A catalogue record is available for this book from the British Library.

Set by ST PAULS
Printed by Melita Press, Malta

ST PAULS is an activity of the priests and brothers
of the Society of St Paul who proclaim the Gospel
through the media of social communication.

CONTENTS

FOREWORD

$\mathcal{W}$ith his Apostolic Letter, *Porta fidei,* Pope Benedict XVI announced a *Year of Faith* beginning on the 11th of October, 2012, the 50th anniversary of the opening of the Second Vatican Council and 20th anniversary of the publication of the *Catechism of the Catholic Church.*

"We want this Year," the Holy Father said, "to arouse in every believer the aspiration to *profess* the faith in fullness and with renewed conviction, with confidence and hope" (*Porta fidei 9*).

In this book, *I believe in One God*, the Pope himself both arouses and satisfies this aspiration! His exploration of the Nicene Creed enables us to rediscover the inexhaustible riches to which the "door of faith" grants us entry. So too, does it inspire us to be credible, joy-filled witnesses to the Risen Lord in today's world, leading many others to cross the threshold of that same "door", not least by our witness of charity. And the Holy Father's presentation of Christian Faith as "a life changing and life sustaining hope" will surely sustain us in our mission until we reach the end of faith's journey – eternal life.

I very much welcome, then, the publication of *I believe in One God* by St Pauls Publishing as part of its response to Pope Benedict's invitation to celebrate the *Year of Faith*. However, this stimulating book is not just for the *Year of Faith*. Rather it will remain a valuable resource to be turned to time after time even when the *Year* has ended, so that all of the good fruits it is bound to bear may continue to flourish.

+ Vincent Nichols
Archbishop of Westminster

INTRODUCTION

In the Year of Faith the Church will be committed in a special way to reviving and deepening the knowledge of Catholic doctrine. A faith which is dull and dormant tarnishes and deforms the real meaning and authentic content of its everlasting value. One of the main aims of Pope Benedict, as he invites us to pass through the "door of the faith", is to help everyone to learn the faith once more so as to live it with an increased awareness and maturity.

In the Pastoral *Note* of the Congregation for the Doctrine of the Faith there is a clear indication of the various events that will celebrate the Year of Faith. It is a time to re-evangelise believers so that they can evangelise and proclaim to others the Christ met in faith. The *Note* tells us that this is an ideal time "for a more attentive reception of the homilies, catechesis, addresses, and documents of the Holy Father", through which we are guided to live the Creed we profess.

To have faith in God is the starting point. One of the tragedies of modern society is the lack of recognition, the loss, or the exclusion of the supremacy of God. The first article of the Creed, on the contrary, puts it as the beginning of everything. It is the source of all the truths about man, who receives from God meaning and direction for his life. It offers him the great hope of the life to come. All that exists in the universe has its origin in Him and returns to Him. Man is not an accidental product of evolution, but the living sign of the power and majesty of God, the free and rational fruit of the Word that was in the beginning. Whoever lives without knowledge of, or orientation towards, God cuts himself off from the source of life.

God has made Himself visible and comes close through the Love that is His very essence, as John tells us (1 Jn 4:8-16) and as the title of the first Encyclical of Benedict XVI, *Deus caritas est* proclaims. The Christian image of God and the consequent image of man are not simply theological and philosophical speculations. God manifested Himself and acted in Jesus Christ, His only begotten Son. He incarnated the truth of the Father and revealed God's love for us. Thereby being the guiding star in the life of men, to lead them to the truth about themselves.

To seek God in the human face of Christ is to seek the truth about God. This truth has its origin in love and leads us to love others. In Benedict XVI's theology of faith, truth and love are always united: one finds its strength in the other and together they are the key to the mystery of creation, to the story of salvation and the mission of the Church. This is the heart of his message and of the Creed also. As the Holy Father has said, "God", "Christ" and "Love" form a harmonious circle. Each is found in the other. The *Logos* of Truth opens and joins the minds of men in the *Logos* of Love, and this is the very essence of the Christian faith. The more we grow in the Truth of God, the more we remain in His love.

God enters the story of humanity as a baby, sharing with men their life situation but without sin. True God and true man, Jesus announces the Kingdom of God and calls everyone to repent so as to enable them to come under His Reign. At the end of His mission the plan of salvation is fulfilled by Jesus' passion, death and resurrection, which are the core of the Creed. The Cross – symbol of suffering and love, forgiveness and reconciliation – becomes the new "rainbow of God" that joins heaven to earth; it drives away the darkness of night and looks forward to the dawn of Easter.

The cross and resurrection are the moment when the earthly life of Christ reaches its climax. They are not only the central and crucial truth of the faith, but also the beginning of a new era in history. Raised forever from the underworld, Jesus returns as a living person to encounter men. The apostles and first disciples spread the proclamation of this extraordinary event: the tomb is empty and Jesus appears to his people. When he goes up to heaven they do not feel lonely and abandoned. Benedict XVI notices, in his second volume of *Jesus of Nazareth*, they are now confident that the Risen One is lifted up "at the right hand of the Father" and will always be with them in a new way.

The Kingdom of God, a universal Kingdom of love, justice and peace, begins a new existence for man who is now reconciled, redeemed and made whole in Christ. From the mystery of Easter are born the need, the enthusiasm and the joy of testifying to the world the greatness of this cosmic event. After Easter, the faith of the disciples is transformed into a faith which is passionate, mature and courageous, making them true imitators of Jesus.

The Holy Spirit breathes life into creation and history, directs it in goodness and beauty, and is the bridge between God and Jesus. He "has spoken through the prophets", whose prophesies in the Old Testament were inspired by Him and in the New Testament were fully accomplished in Christ. The "Come Holy Spirit" is a prayer that proclaims real faith in a living presence, which sustains the new course of the work of God started with the resurrection of Christ. The Holy Spirit is indeed the cement of the unity in the community of the church. The missionaries of the Gospel are fortified and consoled by the permanent reality of the Spirit, who guides them and leads them to the whole truth, giving them the courage to announce it without fear to the end of the earth.

The Holy Spirit acts in each Christian so as to "kindle in the world the wind and breathe of a new Pentecost", which is the reality of the union between the Triune God and the community of believers. The Twelve united together at the Last Supper are in a sense the foundation of the church, the sign of the desire of Jesus to create the new family of God. This family will extend His mission to every age and to every corner of the earth, guided and sustained by the Holy Spirit. The Church echoes the message of the One who became one of us and is always with us. In the Eucharist this presence is visible and all embracing: Christ gives himself.

The Virgin Mary watches over the Church. She was chosen to be the Mother of the Redeemer and therefore Mother of the Church. The real meaning of the church is personified in Mary in her double role as virgin and mother. Her virginity and her motherhood join her to Christ and to his community. The Second Vatican Council and teachings of Paul VI and John Paul II shed light on the role of Mary as the figure and the model by which we can learn to welcome the will of God and by imitating her lowly, humble and courageous faith become the "abode of God". As Pope Benedict says, "Everything in the Church, every institution and department, also the Pope and his successors, are under the mantle of the Virgin Mary". In Mary's unconditional "Yes" to God is manifested the obedience and the courage that are the vocation of every Christian.

The Sacraments are the doorway to the faith and to the life in the Church. At the centre is the Eucharist, "the Sacrament of charity". The faith of the Church is essentially Eucharistic and receives its nourishment from the Eucharist. In every celebration God reveals, carries out and renews his plan of love for the salvation of the world. According to the definition of Thomas of Aquinas, all the other Sacraments point towards and are centred on the Eucharist. They represent the beating heart of the Church. Benedict XVI illustrates the meaning and the distinguishing traits of each of them. He explains their symbolism and the place they occupy at the various moments of the Christian's life.

All this portrays the Christian faith and the hope of eternal life, when "the Divine embraces us and we embrace the Divine". Herein resides the tension of our faith: for by "evangelizing death" faith goes beyond doubts, fears and all the superstitions attached to the "here and now" of the world, and opens us to the immensity of the eternal life in Christ. The goal that gives sense to our journey of faith is this expectation of eternal life, promised to whoever believes in the Son of God (Jn 3:36). Eternal life gives full meaning to death.

From this catechesis on the Creed, we can understand Pope Benedict's theological significance and spiritual inspiration. He wants to be personally involved in the transmission of the authentic treasure of the faith, to both believers and non-believers. This he does in the light of the "new evangelization" of our modern society. He has very often concentrated his attention on the loss of the sense of God, on secularization and relativism, the break between the Gospel and culture, the closure of science and the modern mind to the reasonableness of faith. These issues hinder the knowledge and the practice of the Christian faith. The aim of the Year of Faith is therefore to start anew the work of formation and the re-education of the faithful to the Christian way of living. His hope is that as a result Christ and his Gospel will once again be a spontaneous and visible source of unity in the lives of everyone.

Giuliano Vigini

THE FATHER

The source of all truth

"I ask not only on behalf of these, but also on behalf of those who will believe in me through them" (Jn 17:20). These words Jesus addressed to the Father in the Upper Room. He intercedes for coming generations of believers. He looks beyond the Upper Room, towards the future. He also prayed for us. And he prayed for our unity. This prayer of Jesus is not simply something from the past. He stands before the Father, forever making intercession for us. At this moment he also stands in our midst and he desires to draw us into his own prayer. In the prayer of Jesus we find the very heart of our unity. We will become one if we allow ourselves to be drawn into this prayer. Whenever we gather in prayer as Christians, Jesus' concern for us, and his prayer to the Father for us, ought to touch our hearts. The more we allow ourselves to be drawn into this event, the more we grow in unity.

Did Jesus' prayer go unheard? The history of Christianity is in some sense the visible element of this drama in which Christ strives and suffers with us human beings. Ever anew he must endure the rejection of unity, yet ever anew unity takes place with him and thus with the triune God. We need to see both things: the sin of human beings, who reject God and withdraw within themselves, but also the triumphs of God, who upholds the Church despite her weakness, constantly drawing men and women closer to himself and thus to one another. […]

Our fundamental unity comes from the fact that we believe in God, the Father Almighty, the maker of heaven and earth. And that we confess that he is the triune God – Father, Son and Holy Spirit. The highest unity is not the solitude of a monad, but rather a unity born of love. We believe in God – the real God. We believe that God spoke to us and became one of us. To bear witness to this living God is our common task at the present time.

Does man need God, or can we do quite well without him? When, in the first phase of God's absence, his light continues to illumine and sustain the order of human existence, it appears that things can also function quite well without God. But the more the world withdraws from God, the clearer it becomes that man, in his hubris of power, in his emptiness of heart and in his longing for satisfaction and happiness, increasingly loses his life. A thirst for the infinite is indelibly present in human beings. Man was created to have a relationship with God; we need him. Our primary ecumenical service at this hour must be to bear common witness to the presence of the living God and in this way to give the world the answer which it needs. Naturally, an absolutely central part of this fundamental witness to God is a witness to Jesus Christ, true man and true God, who lived in our midst, suffered and died for us and, in his resurrection, flung open the gates of death.

One God

There is only one God, the Creator of heaven and earth, who is thus the God of all. Two facts are significant about this statement: all other gods are not God, and the universe in which we live has its source in God and was created by him. Certainly, the notion of creation is found elsewhere, yet only here does it become absolutely clear that it is not one god among many, but the one true God himself who is the source of all that exists; the whole world comes into existence by the power of his creative Word. Consequently, his creation is dear to him, for it was willed by him and "made" by him. The second important element now emerges: this God loves man. The divine power that Aristotle at the height of Greek philosophy sought to grasp through reflection, is indeed for every being an object of desire and of love – and as the object of love this divinity moves the world[1] – but in itself it lacks nothing and does not love: it is solely the object of love. The one God in whom Israel believes, on the other hand, loves with a personal love. His love, moreover, is an elective love: among all the nations he chooses Israel and loves her – but he does so precisely with a view to healing the whole human race. God loves, and his love may certainly be called *eros*, yet it is also totally *agape*.[2]

Creator of heaven and earth

The journey along the paths of sacred Scripture begins with the account of creation. This is the liturgy's way of telling us that the creation story is itself a prophecy. It is not information about the external processes by which the cosmos and man himself came into being. The Fathers of the Church were well aware of this. They did not interpret the story as an account of the process of the origins of things, but rather as a pointer towards the essential, towards the true beginning and end of our being. Now, one might ask: is it really important to speak also of creation during the Easter Vigil? Could we not begin with the events in which God calls man, forms a people for himself and creates his history with men upon the earth? The answer has to be: no. To omit the creation would be to misunderstand the very history of God with men, to diminish it, to lose sight of its true order of greatness. The sweep of history established by God reaches back to the origins, back to creation. Our profession of faith begins with the words: "We believe in God, the Father Almighty, Creator of heaven and earth". If we omit the beginning of the *Credo*, the whole history of salvation becomes too limited and too small. The Church is not some kind of association that concerns itself with man's religious needs but is limited to that objective. No, she brings man into contact with God and thus with the source of all things. Therefore we relate to God as Creator, and so we have a responsibility for creation. Our responsibility extends as far as creation because it comes from the Creator. Only because God created everything can he give us life and direct our lives. Life in the Church's faith involves more than a set of feelings and sentiments and perhaps moral obligations. It embraces man in his entirety, from his origins to his eternal destiny. Only because creation belongs to God can we place ourselves completely in his hands. And only because he is the Creator can he give us life forever. Joy over creation, thanksgiving for creation and responsibility for it all belong together.

The central message of the creation account can be defined more precisely still. In the opening words of his Gospel, Saint John sums up the essential meaning of that account in this single statement: "In the beginning was the Word". In effect, the creation account that we listened to earlier is characterized by the regularly recurring phrase: "And God said ..." The world is a product of the Word, of the *Logos*, as Saint John expresses it, using a key term from the Greek language. "*Logos*" means "reason", "sense", "word". It is not reason pure and simple, but creative Reason, that speaks and communicates itself. It is Reason that both is and creates sense. The creation account tells us, then, that the world is a product of creative Reason.

Hence it tells us that, far from there being an absence of reason and freedom at the origin of all things, the source of everything is creative Reason, love, and freedom. Here we are faced with the ultimate alternative that is at stake in the dispute between faith and unbelief: are irrationality, lack of freedom and pure chance the origin of everything, or are reason, freedom and love at the origin of being? Does the primacy belong to unreason or to reason? This is what everything hinges upon in the final analysis.

As believers we answer, with the creation account and with Saint John, that in the beginning is reason. In the beginning is freedom. Hence it is good to be a human person. It is not the case that in the expanding universe, at a late stage, in some tiny corner of the cosmos, there evolved randomly some species of living being capable of reasoning and of trying to find rationality within creation, or to bring rationality into it. If man were merely a random product of evolution in some place on the margins of the universe, then his life would make no sense or might even be a chance of nature. But no, Reason is there at the beginning: creative, divine Reason. And because it is Reason, it also created freedom; and because freedom can be abused, there also exist forces harmful to creation. Hence a thick black line, so to speak, has been drawn across the structure of the universe and across the nature of man. But despite this contradiction, creation itself remains good, life remains good, because at the beginning is good Reason, God's creative love. Hence the world can be saved. Hence we can and must place ourselves on the side of reason, freedom and love – on the side of God who loves us so much that he suffered for us, that from his death there might emerge a new, definitive and healed life.

The Old Testament account of creation that we listened to clearly indicates this order of realities. But it leads us a further step forward. It has structured the process of creation within the framework of a week leading up to the Sabbath, in which it finds its completion. For Israel, the Sabbath was the day on which all could participate in God's rest, in which man and animal, master and slave, great and small were united in God's freedom. Thus the Sabbath was an expression of the Covenant between God and man and creation. In this way, communion between God and man does not appear as something extra, something added later to a world already fully created. The Covenant, communion between God and man, is inbuilt at the deepest level of creation. Yes, the Covenant is the inner ground of creation, just as creation is the external presupposition of the Covenant. God made the world so that there could be a space where he might communicate his love, and from which the response of love might come back to him. From God's perspective, the heart of the man who responds to him is greater and more important than the whole immense material cosmos, for all that the latter allows us to glimpse something of God's grandeur.

The language of creation

In nature, the believer recognizes the wonderful result of God's creative activity, which we may use responsibly to satisfy our legitimate needs, material or otherwise, while respecting the intrinsic balance of creation. If this vision is lost, we end up either considering nature an untouchable taboo or, on the contrary, abusing it. Neither attitude is consonant with the Christian vision of nature as the fruit of God's creation.

Nature expresses a design of love and truth. It is prior to us, and it has been given to us by God as the setting for our life. Nature speaks to us of the Creator (cf. Rom 1:20) and his love for humanity. It is destined to be "recapitulated" in Christ at the end of time (cf. Eph 1:9-10; Col 1:19-20). Thus it too is a "vocation"[3]. Nature is at our disposal not as "a heap of scattered refuse"[4], but as a gift of the Creator who has given it an inbuilt order, enabling man to draw from it the principles needed in order "to till it and keep it" (Gen 2:15). But it should also be stressed that it is contrary to authentic development to view nature as something more important than the human person. This position leads to attitudes of neo-paganism or a new pantheism – human salvation cannot come from nature alone, understood in a purely naturalistic sense. This having been said, it is also necessary to reject the opposite position, which aims at total technical dominion over nature, because the natural environment is more than raw material to be manipulated at our pleasure; it is a wondrous work of the Creator containing a "grammar" which sets forth ends and criteria for its wise use, not its reckless exploitation.

The great hope

It is true that anyone who does not know God, even though he may entertain all kinds of hopes, is ultimately without hope, without the great hope that sustains the whole of life (cf. Eph 2:12). Man's great, true hope which holds firm in spite of all disappointments can only be God – God who has loved us and who continues to love us "to the end," until all "is accomplished" (cf. Jn 13:1 and 19:30). Whoever is moved by love begins to perceive what "life" really is. He begins to perceive the meaning of the word of hope that we encountered in the Baptismal Rite: from faith I await "eternal life" – the true life which, whole and unthreatened, in all its fullness, is simply life. Jesus, who said that he had come so that we might have life and have it in its fullness, in abundance (cf. Jn 10:10), has also explained to us what "life" means: "this is eternal life, that they know you the only true God, and Jesus Christ whom you have sent" (Jn 17:3). Life in its true sense is not something we have exclusively in or from ourselves: it is a relationship. And life in its totality is a relationship with him who is the source of life. If we are in relation with him who does not die, who is Life itself and Love itself, then we are in life. Then we "live".

23

The two dimensions of love

Can we love God without seeing him? And can love be commanded? Against the double commandment of love these questions raise a double objection. No one has ever seen God, so how could we love him? Moreover, love cannot be commanded; it is ultimately a feeling that is either there or not, nor can it be produced by the will. Scripture seems to reinforce the first objection when it states: "If anyone says, 'I love God,' and hates his brother, he is a liar; for he who does not love his brother whom he has seen, cannot love God whom he has not seen" (1 Jn 4:20). But this text hardly excludes the love of God as something impossible. On the contrary, the whole context of the passage quoted from the First Letter of John shows that such love is explicitly demanded. The unbreakable bond between love of God and love of neighbour is emphasized. One is so closely connected to the other that to say that we love God becomes a lie if we are closed to our neighbour or hate him altogether. Saint John's words should rather be interpreted to mean that love of neighbour is a path that leads to the encounter with God, and that closing our eyes to our neighbour also blinds us to God.

True, no one has ever seen God as he is. And yet God is not totally invisible to us; he does not remain completely inaccessible. God loved us first, says the Letter of John quoted above (cf. 4:10), and this love of God has appeared in our midst. He has become visible in as much as he "has sent his only Son into the world, so that we might live through him" (1 Jn 4:9). God has made himself visible: in Jesus we are able to see the Father (cf. Jn 14:9). Indeed, God is visible in a number of ways. In the love-story recounted by the Bible, he comes towards us, he seeks to win our hearts, all the way to the Last Supper, to the piercing of his heart on the Cross, to his appearances after the Resurrection and to the great deeds by which, through the activity of the Apostles, he guided the nascent Church along its path. Nor has the Lord been absent from subsequent Church history: he encounters us ever anew, in the men and women who reflect his presence, in his word, in the sacraments, and especially in the Eucharist. In the Church's Liturgy, in her prayer, in the living community of believers, we experience the love of God, we perceive his presence and we thus learn to recognize that presence in our daily lives. He has loved us first and he continues to do so; we too, then, can respond with love. God does not demand of us a feeling which we ourselves are incapable of producing. He loves us, he makes us see and experience his love, and since he has "loved us first", love can also blossom as a response within us.

In the gradual unfolding of this encounter, it is clearly revealed that love is not merely a sentiment. Sentiments come and go. A sentiment can be a marvellous first spark, but it is not the fullness of love. Earlier we spoke of the process of purification and maturation by which *eros* comes fully into its own, becomes love in the full meaning of the word. It is characteristic of mature love that it calls into play all man's potentialities; it engages the whole man, so to speak. Contact with the visible manifestations of God's love can awaken within us a feeling of joy born of the experience of being loved. But this encounter also engages our will and our intellect. Acknowledgment of the living God is one path towards love, and the "yes" of our will to his will unites our intellect, will and sentiments in the all- embracing act of love. But this process is always open-ended; love is never "finished" and complete; throughout life, it changes and matures, and thus remains faithful to itself. *Idem velle atque idem nolle*[5] – to want the same thing, and to reject the same thing – was recognized by antiquity as the authentic content of love: the one becomes similar to the other, and this leads to a community of will and thought. The love-story between God and man consists in the very fact that this communion of will increases in a communion of thought and sentiment, and thus our will and God's will increasingly coincide: God's will is no longer for me an alien will, something imposed on me from without by the commandments, but it is now my own will, based on the realization that God is in fact more deeply present to me than I am to myself.[6] Then self-abandonment to God increases and God becomes our joy (cf. Ps 73 [72]:23-28).

Love of neighbour is thus shown to be possible in the way proclaimed by the Bible, by Jesus. It consists in the very fact that, in God and with God, I love even the person whom I do not like or even know. This can only take place on the basis of an intimate encounter with God,

an encounter which has become a communion of will,
even affecting my feelings. Then I learn to look on this
other person not simply with my eyes and my feelings,
but from the perspective of Jesus Christ. His friend is my
friend. Going beyond exterior appearances, I perceive in
others an interior desire for a sign of love, of concern.
This I can offer them not only through the organizations
intended for such purposes, accepting it perhaps as a
political necessity. Seeing with the eyes of Christ, I can
give to others much more than their outward necessities;
I can give them the look of love which they crave. Here
we see the necessary interplay between love of God and
love of neighbour which the First Letter of John speaks of
with such insistence. If I have no contact whatsoever with
God in my life, then I cannot see in the other anything
more than the other, and I am incapable of seeing in him
the image of God. But if in my life I fail completely to
heed others, solely out of a desire to be "devout" and to
perform my "religious duties", then my relationship with
God will also grow arid. It becomes merely "proper", but
loveless. Only my readiness to encounter my neighbour
and to show him love makes me sensitive to God as well.
Only if I serve my neighbour can my eyes be opened
to what God does for me and how much he loves me.
The saints – consider the example of Blessed Teresa of
Calcutta – constantly renewed their capacity for love
of neighbour from their encounter with the Eucharistic
Lord, and conversely this encounter acquired its realism

and depth in their service to others. Love of God and love of neighbour are thus inseparable, they form a single commandment. But both live from the love of God who has loved us first. No longer is it a question, then, of a "commandment" imposed from without and calling for the impossible, but rather of a freely-bestowed experience of love from within, a love which by its very nature must then be shared with others. Love grows through love. Love is "divine" because it comes from God and unites us to God; through this unifying process it makes us a "we" which transcends our divisions and makes us one, until in the end God is "all in all" (1 Cor 15:28).

Endnotes

1. Cf. *Metaphysics*, XII, 7.
2. Cf. Ps.-Dionysius the Areopagite, who in his treatise *The Divine Names*, IV, 12-14: PG 3, 709-713 calls God both *eros* and *agape*.
3. John Paul II, *Message for the 1990 World Day of Peace*, 6: *AAS* 82 (1990), 150.
4. Heraclitus of Ephesus (Ephesus, c. 535 B.C. – c. 475 B.C.), Fragment 22B124, in H. Diels and W. Kranz, *Die Fragmente der Vorsokratiker*, Weidmann, Berlin, 1952, 6(th) ed.
5. Sallust, *De coniuratione Catilinae*, XX, 4.
6. Cf. Saint Augustine, *Confessions*, III, 6, 11: CCL 27, 32.

JESUS CHRIST

The revelation of God's love

"They shall look on him whom they have pierced" (Jn 19: 37). This is the biblical theme that this year guides our Lenten reflection. Lent is a favourable time to learn to stay with Mary and John, the beloved disciple, close to him who on the Cross consummated for all mankind the sacrifice of his life (cf. Jn 19:25). With a more fervent participation let us direct our gaze, therefore, in this time of penance and prayer, at Christ Crucified who, dying on Calvary, revealed fully for us the love of God. In the Encyclical *Deus caritas est*, I dwelt upon this theme of love, highlighting its two fundamental forms: *agape* and *eros*.

The term *agape*, which appears many times in the New Testament, indicates the self-giving love of one who looks exclusively for the good of the other. The word *eros*, on the other hand, denotes the love of one who desires to possess what he or she lacks and yearns for union with the beloved. The love with which God surrounds us is undoubtedly *agape*. Indeed, can man give to God some good that he does not already possess? All that the human creature is and has is divine gift. It is the creature, then, who is in need of God in everything. But God's love is also *eros*. In the Old Testament, the Creator of the universe manifests toward the people whom he has chosen as his own a predilection that transcends every human motivation. The prophet Hosea expresses this divine passion with daring images such as the love of a man for an adulterous woman (cf. 3:1-3). For his part, Ezekiel, speaking of God's relationship with the people of Israel, is not afraid to use strong and passionate language (cf. 16:1-22). These biblical texts indicate that *eros* is part of God's very Heart: the Almighty awaits the "yes" of his creatures as a young bridegroom that of his bride. Unfortunately, from its very origins, mankind, seduced by the lies of the Evil One, rejected God's love in the illusion of a self-sufficiency that is impossible (cf. Gn 3: 1-7). Turning in on himself, Adam withdrew from that source of life who is God himself, and became the first of "those who through fear of death were subject to lifelong bondage" (Heb 2: 15). God, however, did not give up. On the contrary, man's "no" was the decisive impulse that moved him to manifest his love in all of its redeeming strength.

It is in the mystery of the Cross that the overwhelming power of the Heavenly Father's mercy is revealed in all of its fullness. In order to win back the love of his creature, he accepted to pay a very high price: the Blood of his Only Begotten Son. Death, which for the first Adam was

30

an extreme sign of loneliness and powerlessness, was thus transformed in the supreme act of love and freedom of the new Adam. One could very well assert, therefore, together with St Maximus the Confessor, that Christ "died, if one could say so, divinely, because he died freely" (*Ambigua*, 91, 1056). On the Cross, God's *eros* for us is made manifest. *Eros* is indeed, as Pseudo-Dionysius expresses it, that force which "does not allow the lover to remain in himself but moves him to become one with the beloved" (*De Divinis Nominibus*, IV, 13: PG 3, 712). Is there more "mad *eros*" (N. Cabasilas, *Vita in Cristo*, 648) than that which led the Son of God to make himself one with us even to the point of suffering as his own the consequences of our offences?

Let us look at Christ pierced on the Cross! He is the unsurpassing revelation of God's love, a love in which *eros* and *agape*, far from being opposed, enlighten each other. On the Cross, it is God himself who begs the love of his creature: He is thirsty for the love of every one of us. The Apostle Thomas recognized Jesus as "Lord and God" when he put his hand into the wound of his side. Not surprisingly, many of the saints found in the Heart of Jesus the deepest expression of this mystery of love. One could rightly say that the revelation of God's *eros* toward man is, in reality, the supreme expression of his *agape*. In all truth, only the love that unites the free gift of oneself with the impassioned desire for reciprocity instils a joy which eases the heaviest of burdens. Jesus said: "When I am lifted up from the earth, I will draw all men to myself"

31

(Jn 12:32). The response the Lord ardently desires of us is above all that we welcome his love and allow ourselves to be drawn to him. Accepting his love, however, is not enough. We need to respond to such love and devote ourselves to communicating it to others. Christ "draws me to himself" in order to unite himself to me, so that I learn to love the brothers with his own love.

"They shall look on him whom they have pierced". Let us look with trust at the pierced side of Jesus from which flow "blood and water" (Jn 19:34)! The Fathers of the Church considered these elements as symbols of the Sacraments of Baptism and the Eucharist. Through the water of Baptism, thanks to the action of the Holy Spirit, we are given access to the intimacy of Trinitarian love. In the Lenten journey, memorial of our Baptism, we are exhorted to come out of ourselves in order to open ourselves in trustful abandonment to the merciful embrace of the Father (cf. St John Chrysostom, *Catecheses*, 3, 14ff.). Blood, symbol of the love of the Good Shepherd, flows into us especially in the Eucharistic mystery: "The Eucharist draws us into Jesus' act of self-oblation... we enter into the very dynamic of his self-giving" (Encyclical *Deus caritas est*, n. 13). Let us live Lent, then, as a "Eucharistic" time in which, welcoming the love of Jesus, we learn to spread it around us with every word and deed. Contemplating "him whom they have pierced" moves us in this way to open our hearts to others, recognizing the wounds inflicted upon the dignity of the human person; it moves us in particular to fight every form of contempt for

life and human exploitation and to alleviate the tragedies of loneliness and abandonment of so many people.

King of the poor and king of peace

To understand what happens on Palm Sunday and to know what this means, not only for that hour but for all time, one detail has proved to be important; it also became the key to understanding the event for his disciples too, when they looked back after Easter with new eyes at those tumultuous days. Jesus entered the Holy City riding on a donkey, that is, the animal of the simple, common country people, and moreover, it was an ass that did not belong to him but one he had asked to borrow for the occasion. He did not arrive in an ostentatious royal carriage or on horseback like the great figures of the world, but on a borrowed donkey. John tells us that at first the disciples did not understand his action. Only after Easter did they realize that Jesus, by so acting, was fulfilling what the prophets had foretold: that his action derived from God's Word and was bringing it to fulfilment. It should be remembered, John said, that in the Book of the Prophet Zechariah we read: "Fear not, daughter of Zion; behold, your king is coming, sitting on the colt of an ass" (Jn 12:15; cf. Zec 9:9). To understand the significance of the prophecy and, consequently, of Jesus' behaviour, we must listen to the whole of Zechariah's text, which continues thus: "He shall banish the chariot from Ephraim, and the horse from Jerusalem; the warrior's bow shall be banished, and he shall proclaim peace to the nations. His dominion will be from sea to sea, and from the river to the ends of the earth" (cf. 9:10). With that, the Prophet says three things about the future king.

In the first place he says that he will be a king of the poor, a poor man among the poor and for the poor. In this case poverty is meant in the sense of the *anawim* of Israel, of those believing and trusting souls that we meet around Jesus – in the perspective of the first Beatitude of the Sermon on the Mount. A person can be materially poor yet his heart can be full of greed for wealth and for the power that derives from it. The very fact that he lives with envy and covetousness shows that, in his heart, he is one of the rich. He wants to reverse the division of goods so that he himself can take over the situation that was previously theirs. The poverty that Jesus means – that the prophets mean – presupposes above all inner freedom from the greed for possession and the mania for power. This is a greater reality than merely a different distribution of possessions, which would still be in the material domain and thereby make hearts even harder. It is first and foremost a matter of purification of heart, through which one recognizes possession as responsibility, as a duty towards others, placing oneself under God's gaze and letting oneself be guided by Christ, who from being rich became poor for our sake (cf. 2 Cor 8:9). Inner freedom is the prerequisite for overcoming the corruption and greed that devastate the world today. This freedom can only be found if God becomes our richness; it can only be found in the patience of daily sacrifices, in which, as it were, true freedom develops. It is the King who points out to us the way to this goal: Jesus, whom we acclaim on Palm Sunday, whom we ask to take us with him on his way.

The second thing the prophet shows us is that this king will be a king of peace: he will cause chariots of war and war horses to vanish, he will break bows and proclaim peace. This is brought about in Jesus through the sign of the Cross. The Cross is the broken bow, in a certain way, God's new, true rainbow which connects the heavens and the earth and bridges the abysses between the continents. The new weapon that Jesus places in our hands is the Cross – a sign of reconciliation, of forgiveness, a sign of love that is stronger than death. Every time we make the Sign of the Cross we should remember not to confront injustice with other injustice or violence with other violence: let us remember that we can only overcome evil with good and never by paying evil back with evil.

The third affirmation of the prophet is the preannouncement of universality. Zechariah says that the kingdom of the king of peace extends "from sea to sea... to the ends of the earth". The ancient promise of the earth, made to Abraham and to the Fathers, is replaced here by a new vision: the domain of the Messianic King is no longer a specific country that would later necessarily be separated from other countries and hence, inevitably, would take a stance against them. His country is the earth, the whole world. He creates unity in the multiplicity of cultures, overcoming every boundary. By perceptively penetrating the clouds of history that separated the Prophet from Jesus, we see in this prophecy, emerging from the distant horizon of prophecy, the network of Eucharistic communities that embraces the earth, the whole world – a network of communities that constitutes Jesus' "Kingdom of peace", which extends from sea to sea, to the ends of the earth. He comes in all cultures and all parts of the world, everywhere, in wretched huts and in poor rural areas as well as in the splendour of cathedrals. He is the same everywhere, the One, and thus all those gathered with him in prayer and communion are also united in one body. Christ rules by making himself our Bread and giving himself to us. It is in this way that he builds his Kingdom.

He suffered under Pontius Pilate

With the Mass *in Coena Domini,* the solemn liturgical rites will help us to meditate more vividly on the Passion, death and Resurrection of the Lord in the days of the Holy Triduum of Easter, the cornerstone of the entire liturgical year. May divine grace open our hearts to an understanding of the invaluable gift of salvation, obtained for us by Christ's sacrifice. We find this immense gift wonderfully described in a famous hymn contained in the Letter to the Philippians (cf. 2:6-11), upon which we have meditated several times during Lent. The Apostle concisely and effectively retraces the mystery of the history of salvation, mentioning the arrogance of Adam who, although he was not God, wanted to be like God. And he compares the arrogance of the first man, which we all tend to feel in our being, with the humility of the true Son of God who, in becoming man does not hesitate to take upon himself all human weaknesses, save sin, and going even as far as the depths of death. This descent to the ultimate depths of the Passion and death is followed by his exaltation, the true glory, the glory of love which went to the very end. And it is therefore right as St Paul says that "at Jesus' name every knee must bend in the heavens, on the earth and under the earth, and every tongue profess that Jesus Christ is Lord" (*ibid.,* 2:10-11). With these words, St Paul refers to a prophecy of Isaiah in which God says: I am God... to me every knee shall bend in Heaven and on earth (cf. Is 45:23). This, Paul says, applies to Jesus Christ. He truly is, in his humility, in the true greatness of his love, the Lord of the world and before him every knee bends.

How marvellous and at the same time surprising this mystery is! We can never sufficiently meditate on this reality. In spite of being God, Jesus does not want to make his divine prerogative an exclusive possession; he does not want to use his being as God, his glorious dignity and his power, as an instrument of triumph and a sign of remoteness from us. On the contrary, "he empties himself", taking on the wretched and weak human condition. In this regard Paul uses a rather evocative Greek verb to indicate the *kénosis,* this humbling of Jesus'. In Christ the divine form (*morphē*) was hidden beneath the human form, that is, beneath our reality marked by suffering, by poverty, by our human limitations and by death. His radical, true sharing in our nature, a sharing in all things save sin, led him to that boundary which is the sign of our finiteness, death. However, all this was not the fruit of an obscure mechanism or blind fatality: rather, it was his own free choice, through generous adherence to the Father's saving plan. And the death he went to meet, Paul adds, was that of crucifixion, the most humiliating and degrading death imaginable. The Lord of the universe did all this out of love for us: out of love he chose "to empty himself" and make himself our brother; out of love he shared our condition, that of every man and every woman. Theodoret of Cyrus, a great witness of the Oriental tradition, wrote on this subject: "being God and God by nature and having equality with God he did not consider this something great, as do those who have received some honour greater than that which they deserve but, concealing his merits, he chose the most profound humility and took the form of a human being" (*Commentary on the Epistle to the Philippians,* 2:6-7). [...]

In the afternoon Mass, called *in Coena Domini,* the Church commemorates the institution of the Eucharist, the ministerial priesthood and the new Commandment of love that Jesus entrusted to his disciples. St Paul offers one of the oldest accounts of what happened in the Upper Room, on the vigil of the Lord's Passion. "The Lord Jesus", he writes at the beginning of the 50s, on the basis of a text he received from the Lord's own environment, "on the night in which he was betrayed took bread, and after he had given thanks, broke it and said, "This is my body, which is for you. Do this in remembrance of me'. In the same way, after the supper, he took the cup, saying, "This cup is the new covenant in my blood. Do this, whenever you drink it, in remembrance of me'" (1 Cor 11:23-25). These words, laden with mystery, clearly show Christ's will: under the species of the Bread and the Wine, he makes himself present with his body given and his Blood poured out. This is the sacrifice of the new and everlasting covenant offered to all, without distinction of race or culture. It is from this sacramental rite, which he presents to the Church as the supreme evidence of his love, that Jesus makes ministers of his disciples and all those who will continue the ministry through the centuries. Thus, Holy Thursday constitutes a renewed invitation to give thanks to God for the supreme gift of the Eucharist, to receive with devotion and to adore with living faith. For this reason the Church encourages the faithful to keep vigil in the presence of the Blessed Sacrament after the celebration of Holy Mass, recalling the sorrowful hour that Jesus spent in solitude and prayer at Gethsemane, before being arrested and then sentenced to death.

He was crucified, died and was buried

And so we come to Good Friday, the day of the Passion and the Crucifixion of the Lord. Every year, standing in silence before Jesus hanging on the wood of the Cross, we feel how full of love the words were that he spoke on the previous evening during the Last Supper. "This is my blood, of the covenant, which is poured out for many" (Mk 14:24). Jesus wanted to offer his life in sacrifice for the remission of humanity's sins. As it does before the Eucharist, as well as before the Passion and death of Jesus on the Cross, the mystery eludes reason. We are placed before something which, humanly, may appear senseless: a God who is not only made Man, with all the needs of man, who not only suffers to save man, taking upon himself the whole tragedy of humanity, but also dies for man.

Christ's death recalls the accumulated sorrow and evils that weigh upon humanity of every age: the crushing weight of our death, the hatred and violence that still today stain the earth with blood. The Passion of the Lord continues in the suffering of human beings. As Blaise Pascal has rightly written: "Jesus will be in agony even to the end of the world. We must not sleep during that time" (*Pensées,* 553). If Good Friday is a day full of sorrow, it is therefore at the same time a particularly propitious day to reawaken our faith, to consolidate our hope and courage so that each one of us may carry our cross with humility, trust and abandonment in God, certain of his support and his victory. The liturgy of this day sings: *O Crux, ave, spes unica* Hail, O Cross, our only hope!

This hope is nourished in the great silence of Holy Saturday, in expectation of the Resurrection of Jesus. On this day the Churches are unadorned and no particular liturgical rites are scheduled. The Church keeps vigil in prayer like Mary and with Mary, sharing her same sentiments of sorrow and of trust in God. It is rightly recommended that a prayerful atmosphere be preserved throughout the day, favourable for meditation and reconciliation; the faithful are encouraged to receive the sacrament of Penance, to be able to take part in the Easter festivities truly renewed. The recollection and silence of Holy Saturday will usher us into the night of the solemn Easter Vigil, "mother of all vigils", when the hymn of joy in Christ's Resurrection will burst forth in all the churches and communities. Once again the victory of light over darkness, of life over death will be proclaimed and the Church will rejoice in the encounter with her Lord. Thus we shall enter into the atmosphere of Easter.

On the third day he rose again

"If Christ has not been raised, then our preaching is in vain and your faith is in vain... and you are still in your sins" (1 Cor 15:14-17). With these strong words from the First Letter to the Corinthians, St Paul makes clear the decisive importance he attributes to the Resurrection of Jesus. In this event, in fact, lies the solution to the problem posed by the drama of the Cross. The Cross alone could not explain the Christian faith, indeed it would remain a tragedy, an indication of the absurdity of being. The Paschal Mystery consists in the fact that the Crucified man "was raised on the third day, in accordance with the Scriptures" (1 Cor 15:4), as proto-Christian tradition attests. This is the keystone of Pauline Christology: everything rotates around this gravitational centre. The whole teaching of Paul the Apostle starts *from,* and arrives *at,* the mystery of him whom the Father raised from the dead. The Resurrection is a fundamental fact, almost a prior axiom (cf. 1 Cor 15:12), on the basis of which Paul can formulate his synthetic proclamation (*kerygma*). He who was crucified and who thus manifested God's immense love for man, is risen again, and is alive among us.

It is important to understand the relationship between the proclamation of the Resurrection, as Paul formulates it, and that was in use since the first pre-Pauline Christian communities. Here indeed we can see the importance of the tradition that preceded the Apostle and that he, with great respect and care, desires to pass on in his turn. The text on the Resurrection, contained in chapter 15:1-11 of the First Letter to the Corinthians, emphasizes the connection between "receiving" and "transmitting". St Paul attributes great importance to the literal formulation of the tradition, and at the end of the passage under consideration underlines, "What matters is that I preach what they preach" (1 Cor 15:11), so drawing attention to the oneness of the *kerygma,* of the proclamation for all believers and for those who will proclaim the Resurrection of Christ. The tradition to which he refers is the fount from which to draw. His Christology is never original at the expense of faithfulness to tradition. The *kerygma* of the Apostles always presides over the personal re-elaboration of Paul; each of his arguments moves from common tradition, and in them he expresses the faith shared by all the Churches, which are one single Church. In this way St Paul offers a model for all time of how to approach theology and how to preach. The theologian, the preacher, does not create new visions of the world and of life, but he is at the service of truth handed down, at the service of the real fact of Christ, of the Cross, and of the Resurrection. His task is to help us understand today the reality of "God with us" that lies behind the ancient words, and thus the reality of true life.

We should here be explicit: St Paul, in proclaiming the Resurrection, does not worry about presenting an organic doctrinal exposition he does not wish to write what would effectively be a theological handbook but he approaches the theme by replying to doubts and concrete questions asked of him by the faithful; an unprepared discourse, then, but one full of faith and theological experience. We find here a concentration of the essential: we have been "justified", that is made just, saved, by Christ who *died* and *rose* again for us. Above all else the *fact* of the Resurrection emerges, without which Christian life would be simply in vain. On that Easter morning something extraordinary happened, something new, and at the same time very concrete, distinguished by very precise signs and recorded by numerous witnesses. For Paul, as for the other authors of the New Testament, the Resurrection is closely bound to the *testimony* of those who had direct experience of the Risen One. This means seeing and hearing, not only with the eyes or with the senses, but also with an interior light that assists the recognition of what the external senses attest as objective fact. Paul gives, therefore, as do the four Gospels, primary importance to the theme of the *appearances*, which constitute a fundamental condition for belief in the Risen One who left the tomb empty. These two facts are important: *the tomb is empty* and *Jesus has in fact appeared.* In this way the links of that tradition were forged, which, through the testimony of the Apostles and the first disciples, was to reach successive generations until it came down to our own. The first consequence, or the first way of expressing this testimony, is to preach the Resurrection of Christ as a synthesis of the Gospel proclamation and as the culminating point in the salvific itinerary. Paul does all this on many occasions: looking at the Letters and the Acts of the Apostles, we can see that for him the essential point is to bear witness to the Resurrection. I should like to cite just one text: Paul, arrested in Jerusalem, stands accused before the Sanhedrin. In this situation, where his life is at stake, he indicates what is the sense and content of all his preaching: "with respect to the hope and the resurrection of the dead I am on trial" (Acts 23:6). This same phrase Paul continually repeats in his Letters (cf. 1 Thes 1:9ff; 4:13-18; 5:10), in which he refers to his own personal experience, to his own meeting with the Risen Christ (cf. Gal 1:15-16, 1 Cor 9:1).

But we may wonder, what, for St Paul, is the deep meaning of the Resurrection of Jesus? What has he to say to us across these 2,000 years? Is the affirmation "Christ is risen" relevant to us today? Why is the Resurrection so important, both for him and for us? Paul gives a solemn answer to this question at the beginning of his Letter to the Romans, where he begins by referring to "the Gospel of God... concerning his Son, who was descended from David according to the flesh, and designated Son of God in power according to the spirit of holiness by his resurrection from the dead" (Rom 1:3-4). Paul knows well, and often says, that Jesus was always the Son of God, from the moment of his Incarnation. The novelty of the Resurrection, consists in the fact that Jesus, raised from the lowliness of his earthly existence, is constituted Son of God "in power". Jesus, humiliated up to the moment of his death on the Cross, can now say to the Eleven, "All authority in heaven and on earth has been given to me" (Mt 28:18). The affirmation of Psalm 2:8 has come to pass. "Ask of me, and I will make the nations your heritage, and the ends of the earth your possession". So, with the Resurrection begins the proclamation of the Gospel of Christ to all peoples the Kingdom of Christ begins, this new Kingdom that knows no power other than that of truth and love. The Resurrection thus reveals definitively the real identity and the extraordinary stature of the Crucified One. An incomparable and towering dignity: *Jesus is God!* For St Paul, the secret identity of Jesus is revealed even more in the mystery of the Resurrection than in the Incarnation. *While the title of Christ*, that is "Messiah"; "the Anointed", in St Paul tends to become the proper name of Jesus, and that of "the *Lord*" indicates his personal relationship with believers, now the title "*Son of God*" comes to illustrate the intimate relationship of Jesus with God, a relationship which is fully revealed in the Paschal event. We can say, therefore, that Jesus rose again to be the Lord of the living and the dead, (cf. Rom 14:9; and 2 Cor 5:15) or in other words, our Saviour (cf. Rom 4:25).

All this bears important consequences for our lives as believers: we are called upon to take part, in our inmost selves, in the whole story of the death and Resurrection of Christ. The Apostle says: we "have died with Christ" and we believe we shall "live with him. For we know that Christ being raised from the dead, will never die again; death no longer has dominion over him" (Rom 6:8-9). This means sharing in the suffering of Christ, which is a prelude to that full unity with him through the resurrection that we hope for. This is also what happened to St Paul, whose personal experience is described in the Letters in tones as sorrowful as they are realistic: "that I may know him and the power of his Resurrection, and may share his sufferings becoming like him in his death, that if possible I may attain the resurrection from the dead" (Phil 3:10-11; cf. 2 Tm 2:8-12). The theology of the Cross is not a theory it is the reality of Christian life. To live in the belief in Jesus Christ, to live in truth and love implies daily sacrifice, implies suffering. Christianity is not the easy road, it is, rather, a difficult climb, but one illuminated by the light of Christ and by the great hope that is born of him. St Augustine says: Christians are not spared suffering, indeed they must suffer a little more, because to live the faith expresses the courage to face in greater depth the problems that life and history present. But only in this way, through the experience of suffering, can we know life in its profundity, in its beauty, in the great hope born from Christ crucified and risen again. The believer, however, finds himself between two poles: on the one hand, the Resurrection, which in a certain sense is already present and operating within us (cf. Col 3:1-4; Eph 2:6); on the other, the urgency to enter into the process which leads everyone and everything towards that fullness described in the Letter to the Romans with a bold image: as the whole of Creation groans and suffers almost as with the pangs of childbirth, so we groan in the expectation of the redemption of our bodies, of our redemption and resurrection (cf. Rom 8:18-23).

He ascended into heaven and is seated at the right hand of the Father

The Word of God highlights Christ's Resurrection, an event that has regenerated believers to a lively hope, as the Apostle Peter states at the beginning of his First Letter.

47

This text constitutes the axis underpinning the itinerary of preparations for this great national meeting. As his Successor, I too exclaim with joy: "Blessed be the God and Father of our Lord Jesus Christ" (1 Pet 1:3), because through the Resurrection of his Son he has regenerated us and has given us by faith the invincible hope of eternal life, so that we live in the present always directed towards the goal, which is the final meeting with our Lord and Saviour. Strengthened by this hope, we are not afraid of trials, which, however painful and heavy, can never impair the profound joy that comes from being loved by God. In his merciful providence, he has given his Son for us and we, even without seeing him, believe in him and love him (cf. 1 Pet 1:3-9). His love is sufficient for us.

Strengthened by this love, firm in faith in the Resurrection of Jesus that builds hope, our Christian witness is born and constantly renewed. It is there that our "Creed" is rooted, the symbol of faith from which the initial preaching was drawn and that continues unaltered to nourish the People of God. The content of the *"kerygma"*, the proclamation, which constitutes the substance of the entire Gospel message, is Christ, the Son of God made Man, who died and rose for us. His Resurrection is the qualifying mystery of Christianity, the superabundant fulfilment of all salvific promises, also those we have heard in the First Reading taken from the end of the Book of the prophet Isaiah. From the Risen Christ, the first fruits of the new humanity, regenerated and regenerating, the "poor" people are truly born, as the prophet foretold, who have opened their hearts to the Gospel and have become and always become new "oaks of righteousness", "the planting of the Lord, that he may be glorified", rebuilders of ruins, restorers of deserted cities, considered by all as the blessed offshoot of the Lord (cf. Is 61:3-4, 9). The mystery of the Resurrection of the Son of God, who, by rising to Heaven is next to the Father, has effused upon us the Holy Spirit and allows us to embrace with a single glance Christ and the Church: the Risen One and the resurrected, the first fruits and the field of God, the cornerstone and the living stones, to use another image from the First Letter of Peter (cf. 2:4-8). So it happened at the beginning with the first apostolic community, and thus it must be even now.

From the day of Pentecost, in fact, the light of the Risen Lord has transfigured the life of the Apostles. They already had the clear perception of not being simply disciples of a new and interesting doctrine, but witnesses chosen and responsible for a revelation linked to the salvation of their contemporaries and all future generations. The Paschal faith filled their hearts with ardour and extraordinary zeal, which made them able to face every difficulty and even death, and impressed their words with an irresistible power of persuasion. Hence, a group of people, lacking human resources and strong by their faith alone, fearlessly faced difficult persecution and martyrdom. The Apostle John writes: "This is the victory that overcomes the world, our faith" (1 Jn 5:4b). The truth of this affirmation is documented also in Italy by two millennia of Christian history, with the countless testimonies of martyrs, saints and blessed. [...]

Today, we are the heirs of those victorious witnesses! But precisely from this observation the question arises: what is our faith? To what extent are we able to communicate it today? The certainty that Christ is risen assures us that no opposition can ever destroy the Church. We are heartened also by the awareness that only Christ can fully satisfy the profound longings of every human heart and respond to the most disturbing questions on pain, injustice and evil, on death and the afterlife. Therefore, our faith is stable, but it is necessary that this faith come alive in each one of us. There is then a vast and capillary effort to be made so that each Christian is transformed into a "witness" ready and able to assume the duty to give a reason to everyone, and always of the hope that is in one (cf. 1 Pet 3:15). To do this, we must return to proclaiming powerfully and joyfully the event of Christ's death and Resurrection, heart of Christianity, principal fulcrum of our faith, powerful lever of our certainty, impetuous wind that sweeps away every fear and indecision, every doubt and human calculation. This decisive change in the world can only come from God. Only starting from the Resurrection can the true nature of the Church and her witness be understood, which is not something detached from the Paschal Mystery but rather is a fruit of it, manifested and accomplished by those who, receiving the Holy Spirit, are sent by Christ to take up his very same mission (cf. Jn 20:21-23).

His kingdom will have no end

On the Solemnity of Christ the King, [...]the last Sunday of the liturgical year and, at the end of the itinerary of faith, presents to us the royal Face of Christ, as the *Pantocrator* in the apse of an ancient basilica.

The primary service of the Successor of Peter is that of the faith. In the New Testament, Peter becomes the "rock" of the Church insofar as he is the bearer of Faith: the "we" of the Church begins with the name of the first man who professed faith in Christ, it begins with *his* faith; a faith that was at first immature and still "too human". Then, however, after Easter it matured and made him capable of following Christ even to the point of giving himself; it developed in the belief that Jesus is truly King; that he is so precisely because he *remained* on the Cross, and *in that way* gave his life for sinners. In the Gospel we see that everyone asks Jesus to come down from the Cross. They mock him, but this is also a way of excusing themselves from blame as if to say: it is not our fault that you are hanging on the Cross; it is solely your fault because if you really were the Son of God, the King of the Jews, you would not stay there but would save yourself by coming down from that infamous scaffold. Therefore, if you remain there it means that you are wrong and we are right. The tragedy that is played out beneath the Cross of Jesus is a universal tragedy; it concerns all people before God who reveals himself for what he is, namely, Love. In the crucified Jesus the divinity is disfigured, stripped of all visible glory and yet is present and real. Faith alone can recognize it: the faith of Mary, who places in her heart too this last scene in the mosaic of her Son's life. She does not yet see the whole, but continues to trust in God, repeating once again with the same abandonment: "Behold, the handmaid of the Lord" (cf. Lk 1:38). Then there is the faith of the Good Thief: a faith barely outlined but sufficient to assure him salvation: "Today you will be with me in Paradise" . This "with me" is crucial. Yes, it is this that saves him. Of course, the good thief is on the cross *like* Jesus, but above all he is on the Cross *with* Jesus. And, unlike the other evildoer and all those who taunt him, he does not ask Jesus to come done from the Cross nor to make him come down. Instead he says: "remember me when you come into your kingdom". The Good Thief sees Jesus on the Cross, disfigured and unrecognizable and yet he entrusts himself to him as to a king, indeed as to the King. The good thief believes what was written on the tablet over Jesus' head: "The King of the Jews". He believed and entrusted himself. For this reason he was already, immediately, in the "today" of God, in Paradise, because Paradise is this: being *with* Jesus, being *with* God. [...]

We know from the Gospels that the Cross was the critical point of the faith of Simon Peter and of the other Apostles. It is clear and it could not be otherwise: they were men and thought "according to men"; they could not tolerate the idea of a crucified Messiah. Peter's "conversion" is fully achieved when he stops wanting "to save" Jesus and accepts to be saved by him. He gives up wanting to save Jesus from the Cross and allows Jesus' Cross to save him. "I have prayed for you that your faith may not fail; and when you have turned again, strengthen your brethren" (Lk 22:32), the Lord says. Peter's ministry consists first of all in his faith, a faith that Jesus immediately recognizes, from the outset, as genuine, as a gift of the heavenly Father; but a faith that must pass through the scandal of the Cross to become authentic, truly "Christian", to become a "rock" on which Jesus can build his Church. Participation in the lordship of Christ is only brought about in practice in the sharing of his self-abasement, with the Cross. My ministry too, dear Brothers, and consequently also yours, consists wholly of faith. Jesus can build his Church on us as long as that true, Paschal faith is found in us, that faith which does not seek to make Jesus come down from the Cross but entrusts itself to him on the Cross. In this regard the true place of the Vicar of Christ is the Cross, it lies in persisting in the obedience of the Cross.

This ministry is difficult because it is not in line with the human way of thinking – with that natural logic which, moreover, continues to be active within us too. But this is and always remains our primary service, the service of faith that transforms the whole of life: believing that Jesus is God, that he is the King precisely *because* he reached that point, because he loved us to the very end. And we must witness and proclaim this paradoxical kingship as he, the King, did, that is, by following his own way and striving to adopt his same logic, the logic of humility and service, of the ear of wheat which dies to bear fruit. The Pope and the Cardinals are called to be profoundly united first of all in this: all together, under the guidance of the Successor of Peter, they must remain in the lordship of Christ, thinking and working in accordance with the logic of the Cross – and this is never easy or predictable. In this we must be united and we are, because it is not an idea or a strategy that unites us but love of Christ and his Holy Spirit. The effectiveness of our service to the Church, the Bride of Christ, depends essentially on this, on our fidelity to the divine kingship of crucified Love. [...]

It is from this that our wisdom derives: *sapientia Crucis*. On this St Paul reflected profoundly. He was the first to outline Christian thought in an organized way, centred precisely on the paradox of the Cross (cf. 1 Cor 1:18-25; 2:1-8). In the Letter to the Colossians, of which today's Liturgy proposes the Christological Hymn – the Pauline reflection, made fertile by the grace of the Spirit, already reaches an impressive level of synthesis in expressing an authentic Christian concept of God and of the world, of personal and universal salvation; and it is all centred on Christ, the Lord of hearts, of history and of the cosmos: "In him the fullness of God was pleased to dwell, and through him to reconcile to himself all things, whether on earth or in Heaven, making peace by the blood of his Cross" (Col 1:19-20). We are always called to proclaim this to the world: Christ "the image of the invisible God", Christ "the first-born of all creation", and "the first-born from the dead", as the Apostle writes, so "that in everything he might be pre-eminent" (Col 1:15, 18). The primacy of Peter and his Successors is totally at the service of this primacy of Jesus Christ, the one Lord; at the service of his Kingdom, that is, of his Kingship of love, so that it might come and be spread, renew men and things, transform the earth and cause peace and justice to germinate in it.

THE HOLY SPIRIT

The Spirit of God

Who or what is the Holy Spirit? How can we recognize him? How do we go to him and how does he come to us? What does he do? The Church's great Pentecostal hymn with which we began Vespers: *"Veni, Creator Spiritus...* Come, Holy Spirit"* gives us a first answer. Here the hymn refers to the first verses of the Bible that describe the creation of the universe with recourse to images. The Bible says first of all that the Spirit of God was moving over the chaos, over the waters of the abyss. The world in which we live is the work of the Creator Spirit. Pentecost is not only the origin of the Church and thus in a special way her feast; Pentecost is also a feast of creation. The world does not exist by itself; it is brought into being by the creative Spirit of God, by the creative Word of God. For this reason Pentecost also mirrors God's wisdom. In its breadth and in the omni-comprehensive logic of its laws, God's wisdom permits us to glimpse something of his Creator Spirit. It elicits reverential awe. Those very people who, as Christians, believe in the Creator Spirit become aware of the fact that we cannot use and abuse the world and matter merely as material for our actions and desires; that we must consider creation a gift that has not been given to us to be destroyed, but to become God's garden, hence, a garden for men and women. In the face of the many forms of abuse of the earth that we see today, let us listen, as it were, to the groaning of creation of which St Paul speaks (Rom 8:22); let us begin by understanding the Apostle's words, that creation waits with impatience for the revelation that we are children of God, to be set free from bondage and obtain his splendour. Dear friends, we want to be these children of God for whom creation is waiting, and we can become them because the Lord has made us such in Baptism. Yes, creation and history – they are waiting for us, for men and women who are truly children of God and behave as such. If we look at history, we see that creation prospered around monasteries, just as with the reawakening of God's Spirit in human hearts the brightness of the Creator Spirit has also been restored to the earth – a splendour that has been clouded and at times even extinguished by the barbarity of the human mania for power. Moreover, the same thing happened once again around Francis of Assisi - it has happened everywhere as God's Spirit penetrates souls, this Spirit whom our hymn describes as light, love and strength. Thus, we have discovered an initial answer to the question as to what the

Holy Spirit is, what he does and how we can recognize him. He comes to meet us through creation and its beauty. However, in the course of human history, a thick layer of dirt has covered God's good creation, which makes it difficult if not impossible to perceive in it the Creator's reflection, although the knowledge of the Creator's existence is reawakened within us ever anew, as it were, spontaneously. [...]

But the Creator Spirit comes to our aid. He has entered history and speaks to us in a new way. In Jesus Christ, God himself was made man and allowed us, so to speak, to cast a glance at the intimacy of God himself. And there we see something totally unexpected: in God, an "I" and a "You" exist. The mysterious God is not infinite loneliness, he is an event of love. If by gazing at creation we think we can glimpse the Creator Spirit, God himself, rather like creative mathematics, like a force that shapes the laws of the world and their order, but then, even, also like beauty – now we come to realize: the Creator Spirit has a heart. He is Love. The Son who speaks to the Father exists and they are both one in the Spirit, who constitutes, so to speak, the atmosphere of giving and loving which makes them one God. This unity of love which is God, is a unity far more sublime than the unity of a last indivisible particle could be. The Triune God himself is the one and only God.

Through Jesus let us as it were cast a glance at God in his intimacy. John, in his Gospel, expressed it like this:

"No one has ever seen God; the only Son, who is in the bosom of the Father, he has made him known" (Jn 1:18). Yet Jesus did not only let us see into God's intimacy; with him, God also emerged, as it were, from his intimacy and came to meet us. This happened especially in his life, passion, death and Resurrection; in his words. Jesus, however is not content with coming to meet us. He wants more. He wants unification. This is the meaning of the images of the banquet and the wedding. Not only must we know something about him, but through him we must be drawn to God. For this reason he had to die and be raised, since he is now no longer to be found in any specific place, but his Spirit, the Holy Spirit, emanates from him and enters our hearts, thereby uniting us with Jesus himself and with the Father, the Triune God.

The Lord, the giver of life

With the testimony of Scripture and Tradition in mind, it is easy to recognize four aspects of the theme of "the Holy Spirit".

First of all there are the words found at the beginning of the Creation account, which speak of the Creator Spirit who sweeps over the face of the abyss, who creates the world and renews it constantly. Faith in the Creator Spirit is an essential part of the Christian creed. The fact that matter has a mathematical structure, is spirit-filled, is the basis of the modern natural sciences. It is only because matter is structured intelligently that our mind can interpret and actively refashion it. The fact that this intelligible structure comes from the same Creator Spirit who also gave us our own spirit, brings with it both a duty and a responsibility. Our faith in creation is the ultimate basis of our responsibility for the earth. The earth is not simply our property, which we can exploit according to our interests and desires. Rather, it is a gift of the Creator, who designed its innate order and has thus given us guidelines which we, as stewards of his creation, need to respect. The fact that the earth and the cosmos mirror the Creator Spirit also means that their rational structures which, beyond their mathematical order, become almost tangible in scientific experimentation, also have an inherent ethical orientation. The Spirit who fashioned them, is more than mathematics – he is Goodness in person who, in and through the language of creation, points out to us the way of an upright life.

Since faith in the Creator is an essential part of the Christian creed, the Church cannot and must not limit herself to passing on to the faithful the message of salvation alone. She has a responsibility towards creation, and must also publicly assert this responsibility. In so doing, she must not only defend earth, water and air as gifts of creation belonging to all. She must also protect man from self-destruction. What is needed is something like a human ecology, correctly understood. If the Church speaks of the nature of the human being as man and woman, and demands that this order of creation be respected, this is not some antiquated metaphysics. What is involved here is faith in the Creator and a readiness to listen to the "language" of creation. To disregard this would be the self-destruction of man himself, and hence the destruction of God's own work. What is often expressed and understood by the term "gender" ultimately ends up being man's attempt at self-emancipation from creation and the Creator. Man wants to be his own master, and alone – always and exclusively – to determine everything that concerns him. Yet in this way he lives in opposition to the truth, in opposition to the Creator Spirit. Rain forests deserve indeed to be protected, but no less so does man, as a creature having an innate "message" which does not contradict our freedom, but is instead its very premise. The great scholastic theologians described marriage, understood as the life-long bond between a man and a woman, as a sacrament of creation, which the Creator himself instituted and which Christ – without modifying the "message" of creation – then made part of the history of his covenant with humanity. An integral part of the Church proclamation must be a witness to the Creator Spirit present in nature as a whole, and, in a special way, in the human person, created in God's image. From this perspective, we should go back to the Encyclical *Humanae Vitae*: the intention of Pope Paul VI was to defend love against sex as a consumer good, the future against the exclusive claims of the present, and human nature against its manipulation.

He has spoken through the Prophets

Let me briefly mention the other dimensions of pneumatology. If the Creator Spirit is manifest first of all in the silent grandeur of the universe, in its intelligent structure, faith also tells us something unexpected: namely, that this Spirit speaks, as it were, with human words, that he entered into history and, as a force that shapes history, is also a Spirit who speaks. Indeed, he is the Word who, in the writings of both the Old and New Testament, comes forth to meet us. In one of his letters, Saint Ambrose expressed marvellously what this means for us: "Even now, as I read the divine Scriptures, God is walking in the Garden" (*Epistulae,* 49, 3). Today, in reading Scripture, we too can, in a sense, roam about the garden of Paradise and encounter God who walks there. The two themes of "the Holy Spirit" and "the Word of God" go hand in hand. In reading Scripture, we learn that Christ and the Holy Spirit are also inseparable. If Paul, with disconcerting conciseness, says: "the Lord is the Spirit" (2 Cor 3:17), he does so not only against the backdrop of the unity of the Son and the Holy Spirit in the life of the Trinity, but also their unity in the history of salvation. In the Passion and Resurrection of Christ, the veil of the merely literal sense is torn away, and the presence of the God who speaks becomes visible. In reading the Scripture with Christ, we learn to hear in human words the voice of the Holy Spirit, and we discover the unity of the Bible.

This now brings us to the third dimension of pneumatology, which consists, precisely, in the inseparability of Christ and the Holy Spirit. This is perhaps most beautifully seen in Saint John's account of the Risen Christ's first appearance to the disciples. The Lord breathes on his disciples, and thus bestows the Holy Spirit upon them. The Holy Spirit is the breath of Christ. And just as the breath of God on the morning of Creation changed the dust of the earth into a living man, so the breath of Christ admits us to ontological communion with the Son, making us a new creation. Hence it is the Holy Spirit who prompts us to say together: "Abba! Father!" (cf. Jn 20:22; Rom 8:15).

The link between Spirit and Church thus naturally emerges as a fourth dimension. In his First Letter to the Corinthians, chapter 12, and in his Letter to the Romans, chapter 12, Paul described the Church as the Body of Christ, and thus as an organism of the Holy Spirit, in which the gifts of the Holy Spirit fuse individuals into a single living whole.

The Holy Spirit is the Spirit of the Body of Christ. In the fullness of this Body we discover our task, we live for one another and in dependence on others, drawing deep life from the One who lived and suffered for us all and who, through his Spirit, draws us to himself in the unity of all God's children. As Augustine says in this regard: "Do you too desire to live from the Spirit of Christ? Then be in the Body of Christ" (*Tract. in Jo.* 26, 13).

Come, Holy Spirit

In the solemn celebration of Pentecost we are invited to profess our faith in the presence and in the action of the Holy Spirit and to invoke his outpouring upon us, upon the Church and upon the whole world. With special intensity, let us make our own the Church's invocation: *Veni, Sancte Spiritus!* It is such a simple and spontaneous invocation, yet also extraordinarily profound, which came first of all from the heart of Christ. The Spirit is indeed the gift that Jesus asked and continues to ask of his Father for his friends; the first and principal gift that he obtained for us through his Resurrection and Ascension into heaven.

The Gospel passage, which has the Last Supper as its context, speaks to us of this prayer of Christ. The Lord Jesus said to his disciples: "If you love me, you will keep my commandments. And I will pray the Father, and he will give you another Counsellor, to be with you for ever" (Jn 14:15-16). Here the praying heart of Jesus is revealed to us, his filial and fraternal heart. This prayer reaches its apex and its fulfilment on the Cross, where Christ's invocation is one with the total gift that he makes of himself, and thus his prayer becomes, so to speak, the very seal of his self-gift out of love of the Father and humanity. Invocation and donation of the Holy Spirit meet, they permeate each other, they become one reality. "And I will pray the Father, and he will give you another Counsellor, to be with you for ever". In reality, Jesus' prayers that

65

of the Last Supper and that on the Cross form a single prayer that continues even in heaven, where Christ sits at the right hand of the Father. Jesus, in fact, always lives his intercessional priesthood on behalf of the people of God and humanity and so prays for all of us, asking the Father for the gift of the Holy Spirit.

The account of Pentecost in the Book of the Acts of the Apostles we listened to in the First Reading (cf. Acts 2: 1-11) presents the "new course" of the work that God began with Christ's Resurrection, a work that involves mankind, history and the cosmos. The Son of God, dead and Risen and returned to the Father, now breathes with untold energy the divine breath upon humanity, the Holy Spirit. And what does this new and powerful self-communication of God produce? Where there are divisions and estrangement the Paraclete creates unity and understanding. The Spirit triggers a process of reunification of the divided and dispersed parts of the human family. People, often reduced to individuals in competition or in conflict with each other, when touched by the Spirit of Christ open themselves to the experience of communion, which can involve them to such an extent as to make of them a new body, a new subject: the Church. This is the effect of God's work: unity; thus unity is the sign of recognition, the "business card" of the Church throughout her universal history. From the very beginning, from the Day of Pentecost, she speaks all languages. The universal Church precedes the particular Churches, and the latter must always conform to the former according to a criterion of unity and universality. The Church never remains a prisoner within political, racial and cultural confines; she cannot be confused with States nor with Federations of States, because her unity is of a different type and aspires to transcend every human frontier.

From this, dear brothers, derives a practical criterion for discerning Christian life: when a person or a community limits itself to its own way of thinking and acting, it is a sign that it has distanced itself from the Holy Spirit. The path of Christians and of the particular Churches must always coincide with the path of the one, catholic Church, and harmonize with it. This does not mean that the unity created by the Holy Spirit is a kind of egalitarianism. On the contrary, that is rather the model of Babel, or in other words, the imposition of a culture characterized by what we could define as "technical" unity. In fact, the Bible tells us (cf. Gen 11:1-9) that in Babel everyone spoke the same language. At Pentecost, however, the Apostles speak different languages in such a way that everyone understands the message in his own tongue. The unity of the Spirit is manifest in the plurality of understanding. The Church is one and multiple by her nature, destined as she is to live among all nations, all peoples, and in the most diverse social contexts. She responds to her vocation to be a sign and instrument of unity of the human race (cf. *Lumen Gentium*, n. 1) only if she remains autonomous from every State and every specific culture. Always and everywhere the Church must truly be catholic and universal, the house of all in which each one can find a place.

The Holy Spirit in the life of the Church

Ecclesial communion is inspired and sustained by the Holy Spirit and preserved and promoted by the apostolic ministry. And this communion, which we call "Church", does not only extend to all believers in a specific historical period, but also embraces all the epochs and all the generations. Thus, we have a twofold universality: a synchronic universality – we are united with believers in every part of the world – and also a so-called diachronic universality, that is: all the epochs belong to us, and all the believers of the past and of the future form with us a single great communion. The Holy Spirit appears to us as the guarantor of the active presence of the mystery in history, the One who ensures its realization down the centuries. Thanks to the Paraclete, it will always be possible for subsequent generations to have the same experience of the Risen One that was lived by the apostolic community at the origin of the Church, since it is passed on and actualized in the faith, worship and communion of the People of God, on pilgrimage through time. And so it is that we today, in the Easter Season, are living the encounter with the Risen One not only as something of the past, but in the present communion of the faith, liturgy and life of the Church. The Church's apostolic Tradition consists in this transmission of the goods of salvation which, through the power of the Spirit makes the Christian community the permanent actualization of the original communion. It is called "original" because it was born of the witness of the Apostles and of the community of the disciples at the time of the origins. It was passed on under the guidance of the Holy Spirit in the New Testament writings and in the sacramental life, in the life of the faith, and the Church continuously refers to it – to this Tradition, which is the whole, ever up-to-date reality of Jesus' gift – as her foundation and her law, through the uninterrupted succession of the apostolic ministry.

In his historical life furthermore, Jesus limited his mission to the house of Israel, but already made it clear that the gift was not only destined for the People of Israel but to everyone in the world and to every epoch. The Risen One then explicitly entrusted to the Apostles (cf. Lk 6:13) the task of making disciples of all the nations, guaranteeing his presence and help to the end of the age (cf. Mt 28:19 ff.). The universalism of salvation, moreover, requires that the Easter memorial be celebrated in history without interruption until Christ's glorious return (cf. 1 Cor 11:26). Who will bring about the saving presence of the Lord Jesus through the ministry of the Apostles – heads of the eschatological Israel (cf. Mt 19:28) – and through the whole life of the people of the New Covenant? The answer is clear: the Holy Spirit. The Acts of the Apostles – in continuity with the pattern of Luke's Gospel – show vividly the interpenetration between the Spirit, those sent out by Christ and the community they have gathered. Thanks to the action of the Paraclete, the Apostles and their successors can realize in time the mission received from the Risen One. "You are witnesses of these things. And behold, I send the promise of my Father upon you" (Lk 24:48 ff.). "You shall receive power when the Holy Spirit has come upon you; and you shall be my witnesses in Jerusalem and in all Judea and Samaria and to the end of the earth" (Acts 1:8). And this promise, which at first seems incredible, already came true in the Apostles' time: "And we are witnesses to these things, and so is the Holy Spirit whom God has given to those who obey him" (Acts 5:32).

So it is the Spirit himself, who through the laying on of hands and prayers of the Apostles, consecrates and sends out new Gospel missionaries (as, for example, in Acts 13:3 ff. and 1 Tm 4:14). It is interesting to observe that whereas in some passages it says that Paul appointed elders in every Church (cf. Acts 14:23), elsewhere it says that it is the Spirit who has made them guardians of the flock (cf. Acts 20:28). The action of the Spirit and the action of Paul thus are deeply interwoven. At the time of solemn decisions for the life of the Church, the Spirit is present to guide her. This guiding presence of the Holy Spirit was particularly acutely felt in the Council of Jerusalem, in whose conclusive words resound the affirmation: "For it has seemed good to the Holy Spirit and to us..." (Acts 15:28); the Church grows and walks "in the fear of the Lord, and in the comfort of the Holy Spirit" (Acts 9:31). This permanent actualization of the active presence of the Lord Jesus in his People, brought about by the Holy Spirit and expressed in the Church through the apostolic ministry and fraternal communion is what, in a theological sense, is meant by the term "Tradition": it is not merely the material transmission of what was given at the beginning to the Apostles, but the effective presence of the Crucified and Risen Lord Jesus who accompanies and guides in the Spirit the community he has gathered together.

Tradition is the communion of the faithful around their legitimate Pastors down through history, a communion that the Holy Spirit nurtures, assuring the connection between the experience of the apostolic faith, lived in the original community of the disciples, and the actual experience of Christ in his Church. In other words, Tradition is the practical continuity of the Church, the holy Temple of God the Father, built on the foundation of the Apostles and held together by the cornerstone, Christ, through the life-giving action of the Spirit: "So then you are no longer strangers and sojourners, but you are fellow citizens with the saints and members of the household of God, built upon the foundation of the apostles and prophets, Christ Jesus himself being the cornerstone, in whom the whole structure is joined together and grows into a holy temple in the Lord; in whom you also are built into it for a dwelling place of God in the Spirit" (Eph 2:19-22). Thanks to Tradition, guaranteed by the ministry of the Apostles and by their successors, the water of life that flowed from Christ's side and his saving blood reach the women and men of all times. Thus, Tradition is the permanent presence of the Saviour who comes to meet us, to redeem us and to sanctify us in the Spirit, through the ministry of his Church, to the glory of the Father.

Concluding and summing up, we can therefore say that Tradition is not the transmission of things or words, a collection of dead things. Tradition is the living river that links us to the origins, the living river in which the origins are ever present, the great river that leads us to the gates of eternity. And since this is so, in this living river the words of the Lord that we heard on the reader's lips to start with are ceaselessly brought about: "I am with you always, to the close of the age" (Mt 28:20).

The breath of christian life

Attentive listening to the Word of God concerning the mystery and action of the Holy Spirit opens us up to great and inspiring insights that I shall summarize in the following points.

Shortly before his Ascension, Jesus said to his disciples: "And behold, I send the promise of my Father upon you" (Lk 24:49). This took place on the day of Pentecost when they were together in prayer in the Upper Room with the Virgin Mary. The outpouring of the Holy Spirit on the nascent Church was the fulfillment of a promise made much earlier by God, announced and prepared throughout the Old Testament.

In fact, right from its opening pages, the Bible presents the spirit of God as the *wind* that "was moving over the face of the waters" (cf. Gen 1:2). It says that God *breathed* into man's nostrils the *breath* of life (cf. Gen 2:7), thereby infusing him with life itself. After original sin, the life-giving spirit of God is seen several times in the history of humankind, calling forth prophets to exhort the chosen people to return to God and to observe his commandments faithfully. In the well-known vision of the prophet Ezekiel, God, with his spirit, restores to life the people of Israel, represented by the "dry bones" (cf. 37:1-14). Joel prophesied an "outpouring of the spirit" over all the people, excluding no one. The sacred author wrote: "And it shall come to pass afterward that I will pour out my spirit on all flesh ... Even upon the menservants and maidservants, in those days, I will pour out my spirit" (3:1-2).

In "the fullness of time" (cf. Gal 4:4), the angel of the Lord announced to the Virgin of Nazareth that the Holy Spirit, "the power of the Most High", would come upon her and overshadow her. The child to be born would be holy and would be called Son of God (cf. Lk 1:35). In the words of the prophet Isaiah, the Messiah would be the one on whom the Spirit of the Lord would rest (cf. 11:1-2; 42:1). This is the prophecy that Jesus took up again at the start of his public ministry in the synagogue in Nazareth. To the amazement of those present, he said: "The Spirit of the Lord is upon me, because he has anointed me to bring good news to the poor. He has sent me to proclaim release to the captives and recovery of sight to the blind, to let the oppressed go free, to proclaim the year of the Lord's favour" (Lk 4:18-19; cf. Is 61:1-2). Addressing those present, he referred those prophetic words to himself by saying: "Today this Scripture has been fulfilled in your hearing" (Lk 4:21). Again, before his death on the Cross, he would tell his disciples several times about the coming of the Holy Spirit, the "Counselor" whose mission would be to bear witness to him and to assist believers by teaching them and guiding them to the fullness of Truth (cf. Jn 14:16-17, 25-26; 15:26; 16:13).

On the evening of the day of resurrection, Jesus appeared to his disciples, "he breathed on them and said to them, 'Receive the Holy Spirit'" (Jn 20:22). With even greater power the Holy Spirit descended on the Apostles on the day of Pentecost. We read in the Acts of the Apostles: "And suddenly from heaven there came a sound like the rush of a violent wind, and it filled the entire house where they were sitting. Divided tongues, as of fire, appeared among them, and a tongue rested on each of them" (2:2-3).

The Holy Spirit *renewed* the Apostles *from within*, filling them with a power that would give them courage to go out and *boldly proclaim* that "Christ has died and is risen!" Freed from all fear, they began to speak openly with *self-confidence* (cf. Acts 2:29; 4:13; 4:29,31). These frightened fishermen had become courageous heralds of the Gospel. Even their enemies could not understand how "uneducated and ordinary men" (cf. Acts 4:13) could show such courage and endure difficulties, suffering and persecution with joy. Nothing could stop them. To those who tried to silence them they replied: "We cannot keep from speaking about what we have seen and heard" (Acts 4:20). This is how the Church was born, and from the day of Pentecost she has not ceased to spread the Good News "to the ends of the earth" (Acts 1:8).

If we are to understand the mission of the Church, we must go back to the Upper Room where the disciples remained together (cf. Lk 24:49), praying with Mary, the "Mother", awaiting the Spirit that had been promised. This icon of the nascent Church should be a constant source of inspiration for every Christian community. Apostolic and missionary fruitfulness is not principally due to programmes and pastoral methods that are cleverly drawn up and "efficient", but is the result of the community's constant prayer (cf. *Evangelii Nuntiandi*, 75). Moreover, for the mission to be effective, communities must be united, that is, they must be "of one heart and soul" (cf. Acts 4:32), and they must be ready to witness to the love and joy that the Holy Spirit instils in the hearts of the faithful (cf. Acts 2:42). The Servant of God John Paul II wrote that, even prior to action, the Church's mission is to witness and to live in a way that shines out to others (cf. *Redemptoris Missio*, 26). Tertullian tells us that this is what happened in the early days of Christianity when pagans were converted on seeing the love that reigned among Christians: "See how they love one another" (cf. *Apology*, 39 § 7).

To conclude this brief survey of the Word of God in the Bible, I invite you to observe how the Holy Spirit is the highest gift of God to humankind, and therefore the supreme testimony of his love for us, a love that is specifically expressed as the "yes to life" that God wills for each of his creatures. This "yes to life" finds its fullness in Jesus of Nazareth and in his victory over evil by means of the redemption. In this regard, let us never forget that the Gospel of Jesus, precisely because of the Spirit, cannot be reduced to a mere statement of fact, for it is intended to be "good news for the poor, release for captives, sight for the blind ...". With what great vitality this was seen on the day of Pentecost, as it became the grace and the task of the Church towards the world, her primary mission! We are the fruits of this mission of the Church through the working of the Holy Spirit. We carry within us the seal of the Father's love in Jesus Christ which is the Holy Spirit. Let us never forget this, because the Spirit of the Lord always remembers every individual, and wishes, particularly through you young people, to stir up the wind and fire of a new Pentecost in the world.

THE CHURCH

Built on the foundation of the Apostles

The Church was built on the foundation of the Apostles as a community of faith, hope and charity. Through the Apostles, we come to Jesus himself. The Church begins to establish herself when some fishermen of Galilee meet Jesus, allowing themselves to be won over by his gaze, his voice, his warm and strong invitation: "Follow me, and I will make you become fishers of men" (Mk 1:17; Mt 4:19). At the start of the third millennium, my beloved Predecessor John Paul II invited the Church to contemplate the Face of Christ (cf. *Novo Millennium Ineunte,* n. 16ff.). Continuing in the same direction, I would like to show, in the Catechesis that I begin today, how it is precisely the light of that Face that is reflected on the face of the Church (cf. *Lumen Gentium,* n. 1), notwithstanding the limits and shadows of our fragile and sinful humanity. After Mary, a pure reflection of the light of Christ, it is from the Apostles, through their word and witness, that we receive the truth of Christ. Their mission is not isolated, however, but is situated within a mystery of communion that involves the entire People of God and is carried out in stages from the Old to the New Covenant.

In this regard, it must be said that the message of Jesus is completely misunderstood if it is separated from the context of the faith and hope of the Chosen People: like John the Baptist, his direct Precursor, Jesus above all addresses Israel (cf. Mt 15:24) in order to "gather" it together in the eschatological time that arrived with him. And like that of John, the preaching of Jesus is at the same time a call of grace and a sign of contradiction and of justice for the entire People of God. And so, from the first moment of his salvific activity, Jesus of Nazareth strives to gather together the People of God. Even if his preaching is always an appeal for personal conversion, in reality he continually aims to build the People of God whom he came to bring together, purify and save. As a result, therefore, an individualistic interpretation of Christ's proclamation of the Kingdom, specific to liberal theology, is unilateral and without foundation, as a great liberal theologian Adolf von Harnack summed it up in the year 1900 in his lessons on *The essence of Christianity:* "The Kingdom of God, insofar as it comes in *single* individuals, is able to enter their soul and is welcomed by them. The Kingdom of God is the *dominion* of God, certainly, but it is the dominion of the holy God in individual hearts" (cf. Third Lesson, 100 ff.). In reality, this individualism of liberal theology is a typically modern accentuation: in the perspective of biblical tradition and on the horizon of Judaism, where the work of Jesus is situated in all its novelty, it is clear that the entire mission of the Son-made-flesh has a communitarian finality. He truly came to unite dispersed humanity; he truly came to unite the People of God.

An evident sign of the intention of the Nazarene to gather together the community of the Covenant, to demonstrate in it the fulfilment of the promises made to the Fathers who always speak of convocation, unification, unity, is *the institution of the Twelve*. We heard about this institution of the Twelve in the Gospel reading. I shall read the central passage again: "And he went up into the hills and called to him those whom he desired; and they came to him. And he appointed twelve to be with him, and to be sent out to preach and have authority to cast out demons. The names of the twelve Apostles are these..." (Mk 3:13-16; cf. Mt 10:1-4; Lk 6:12-16). On the site of the revelation, "the mount", taking initiative that demonstrates absolute awareness and determination, Jesus establishes the Twelve so that, together with him, they are witnesses and heralds of the coming of the Kingdom of God. There are no doubts about the historicity of this call, not only because of the antiquity and multiplicity of witnesses, but also for the simple reason that there is also the name of Judas, the Apostle who betrayed him, notwithstanding the difficulties that this presence could have caused the new community. The number 12, which evidently refers to the 12 tribes of Israel, already reveals the meaning of the prophetic-symbolic action implicit in the new initiative to re-establish the holy people. As the system of the 12 tribes had long since faded out, the hope of Israel awaited their restoration as a sign of the eschatological time (as referred to at the end of the Book of Ezekiel: 37:15-19; 39:23-29; 40-48). In choosing the Twelve, introducing them into a communion of life with himself and involving them in his mission of proclaiming the Kingdom in words and works (cf. Mk 6:7-13; Mt 10:5-8; Lk 9:1-6; 6:13), Jesus wants to say that the definitive time has arrived in which to constitute the new People of God, the people of the 12 tribes, which now becomes a universal people, his Church.

With their very own existence, the Twelve – called from different backgrounds – become an appeal for all of Israel to convert and allow herself to be gathered into the new covenant, complete and perfect fulfilment of the ancient one. The fact that he entrusted to his Apostles, during the Last Supper and before his Passion, the duty to celebrate his Pasch, demonstrates how Jesus wished to transfer to the entire community, in the person of its heads, the mandate to be a sign and instrument in history of the eschatological gathering begun by him. In a certain sense we can say that the Last Supper itself is the act of foundation of the Church, because he gives himself and thus creates a new community, a community united in communion with himself. In this light, one understands how the Risen One confers upon them, with the effusion of the Spirit, the power to forgive sins (cf. Jn 20:23). Thus, the Twelve Apostles are the most evident sign of Jesus' will regarding the existence and mission of his Church, the guarantee that between Christ and the Church there is no opposition: despite the sins of the people who make up the Church, they are inseparable. Therefore, a slogan that was popular some years back: "Jesus yes, Church no", is totally inconceivable with the intention of Christ. This individualistically chosen Jesus is an imaginary Jesus. We cannot have Jesus without the reality he created and in which he communicates himself. Between the Son of God-made-flesh and his Church there is a profound, unbreakable and mysterious continuity by which Christ is present today in his people. He is always contemporary with us, he is always contemporary with the Church, built on the foundation of the Apostles and alive in the succession of the Apostles. And his very presence in the community, in which he himself is always with us, is the reason for our joy. Yes, Christ is with us, the Kingdom of God is coming.

One, holy, catholic and apostolic

The Feast of the Holy Apostles Peter and Paul is at the same time a grateful memorial of the great witnesses of Jesus Christ and a solemn confession for the Church: *one, holy, catholic and apostolic*. It is first and foremost a feast of *catholicity*. The sign of Pentecost – the new community

81

that speaks all languages and unites all peoples into one people, in one family of God -, this sign has become a reality. […]This brings to fulfilment the mission of St Paul, who knew that he was the "minister of Christ Jesus among the Gentiles, with the priestly duty of preaching the Gospel of God so that the Gentiles [might] be offered up as a pleasing sacrifice, consecrated by the Holy Spirit" (Rom 15:16). The purpose of the mission is that humanity itself becomes a living glorification of God, the true worship that God expects: this is the deepest meaning of *catholicity* – a *catholicity* that has already been given to us, towards which we must constantly start out again. *Catholicity* does not only express a horizontal dimension, the gathering of many people in unity, but also a vertical dimension: it is only by raising our eyes to God, by opening ourselves to him, that we can truly become one. Like Paul, Peter also came to Rome, to the city that was a centre where all the nations converged and, for this very reason, could become, before any other, the expression of the universal outreach of the Gospel. As he started out on his journey from Jerusalem to Rome, he must certainly have felt guided by the voices of the prophets, by faith and by the prayer of Israel. The mission to the whole world is also part of the proclamation of the Old Covenant: the people of Israel were destined to be a light for the Gentiles. The great Psalm of the Passion, Psalm 22[21], whose first verse Jesus cried out on the Cross: "My God, my God, why have you forsaken me?", ends with the vision: "All the ends of the earth shall remember and turn to the Lord; all the families of the nations shall bow down before him" (Ps 22[21]:28). When Peter and Paul came to Rome, the Lord on the Cross who had uttered the first line of that Psalm was risen; God's victory now had to be proclaimed to all the nations, thereby fulfilling the promise with which the Psalm concludes.

Catholicity means *universality* – a multiplicity that becomes unity; a unity that nevertheless remains multiplicity. From Paul's words on the Church's *universality* we have already seen that the ability of nations to get the better of themselves in order to look towards the one God, is part of this *unity*. In the second century, the founder of Catholic theology, St Irenaeus of Lyons, described very beautifully this bond between catholicity and unity and I quote him. He says: "The Church spread across the world diligently safeguards this doctrine and this faith, forming as it were one family: the same faith, with one mind and one heart, the same preaching, teaching and tradition as if she had but one mouth. Languages abound according to the region but the power of our tradition is one and the same. The Churches in Germany do not differ in faith or tradition, neither do those in Spain, Gaul, Egypt, Libya, the Orient, the centre of the earth; just as the sun, God's creature, is one alone and identical throughout the world, so the light of true preaching shines everywhere and illuminates all who desire to attain knowledge of the truth" (*Adv. Haer.* I 10, 2). The *unity* of men and women in their multiplicity has become possible because God, this one God of heaven and earth, has shown himself to us; because the essential truth about our lives, our "where from?" and "where to?" became visible when he revealed himself to us and enabled us to see his face, himself, in Jesus Christ. This truth about the essence of our being, living and dying, a truth that God made visible, unites us and makes us brothers and sisters. *Catholicity* and *unity* go hand in hand. And *unity* has a content: the faith that the Apostles passed on to us in Christ's name. [...]

We have said that the *catholicity* of the Church and the *unity* of the Church go together. The fact that both dimensions become visible to us in the figures of the holy Apostles already shows us the consequent characteristic of the Church: she is *apostolic.* What does this mean? The Lord established Twelve Apostles just as the sons of Jacob were 12. By so doing he was presenting them as leaders of the People of God which, henceforth universal, from that time has included all the peoples. St Mark tells us that Jesus called the Apostles so "to be with him, and to be sent out" (Mk 3:14). This seems almost a contradiction in terms. We would say: "Either they stayed with him or they were sent forth and set out on their travels". Pope St Gregory the Great says a word about angels that helps us resolve this contradiction. He says that angels are always sent out and at the same time are always in God's presence, and continues, "Wherever they are sent, wherever they go, they always journey on in God's heart" (*Homily,* 34, 13).

The Book of Revelation described Bishops as "angels" in their Church, so we can state: the Apostles and their successors must always be with the Lord and precisely in this way – wherever they may go – they must always be in communion with him and live by this communion.

The Church is *apostolic,* because she professes the faith of the Apostles and attempts to live it. There is a unity that marks the Twelve called by the Lord, but there is also continuity in the apostolic mission. St Peter, in his First Letter, described himself as "a fellow elder" of the presbyters to whom he writes (5:1). And with this he expressed the principle of apostolic succession: the same ministry which he had received from the Lord now continues in the Church through priestly ordination. The Word of God is not only written but, thanks to the testimonies that the Lord in the sacrament has inscribed in the apostolic ministry, it remains a living word. [...] *Unity* as well as *apostolicity* are bound to the Petrine service that visibly unites the Church of all places and all times, thereby preventing each one of us from slipping into the kind of false autonomy that all too easily becomes particularization of the Church and might consequently jeopardize her independence. So, let us not forget that the purpose of all offices and ministries is basically that "we [all] become one in faith and in the knowledge of God's son, and form that perfect man who is Christ come to full stature", so that the Body of Christ may grow and build "itself up in love" (Eph 4:13,16).

The Gospel tells of the profession of faith of St Peter, on whom the Church was founded: "You are the Messiah... the Son of the living God" (Mt 16:16). Having spoken today of the Church as *one, catholic and apostolic* but not yet of the Church as *holy,* let us now recall another profession of Peter, his response on behalf of the Twelve at the moment when so many abandoned Christ: "We have come to believe; we are convinced that you are God's holy one" (Jn 6:69). What does this mean? Jesus, in his great priestly prayer, says that he is consecrating himself for his disciples, an allusion to the sacrifice of his death (cf. Jn 17:19). By saying this, Jesus implicitly expresses his role as the true High Priest who brings about the mystery of the "Day of Reconciliation", no longer only in substitutive rites but in the concrete substance of his own Body and Blood. The Old Testament term "the Holy One of the Lord" identified Aaron as the High Priest who had the task of bringing about Israel's sanctification (Ps 106[105]:16; Vulgate: Sir 45:6). Peter's profession of Christ, whom he declares to be the Holy One of God, fits into the context of the Eucharistic Discourse in which Jesus announces the Day of Reconciliation through the sacrificial offering of himself: "the bread I will give is my flesh, for the life of the world" (Jn 6:51). So this profession is the background of the priestly mystery of Jesus, his sacrifice for us all. The Church is not *holy* by herself; in fact, she is made up of sinners – we all know this and it is plain for all to see. Rather, she is made holy ever anew by the Holy One of

God, by the purifying love of Christ. God did not only speak, but loved us very realistically; he loved us to the point of the death of his own Son. It is precisely here that we are shown the full grandeur of revelation that has, as it were, inflicted the wounds in the heart of God himself. Then each one of us can say personally, together with St Paul, I live "a life of faith in the Son of God, who loved me and gave himself for me" (Gal 2:20).

Eucharistic community

Through the sacrament of the Eucharist Jesus draws the faithful into his "hour;" he shows us the bond that he willed to establish between himself and us, between his own person and the Church. Indeed, in the sacrifice of the Cross, Christ gave birth to the Church as his Bride and his body. The Fathers of the Church often meditated on the relationship between Eve's coming forth from the side of Adam as he slept (cf. Gen 2:21-23) and the coming forth of the new Eve, the Church, from the open side of Christ sleeping in death: from Christ's pierced side, John recounts, there came forth blood and water (cf. Jn 19:34), the symbol of the sacraments[1]. A contemplative gaze "upon him whom they have pierced" (Jn 19:37) leads us to reflect on the causal connection between Christ's sacrifice, the Eucharist and the Church. The Church "draws her life from the Eucharist"[2]. Since the Eucharist makes present Christ's redeeming sacrifice, we must start by acknowledging that "there is a causal influence of the Eucharist at the Church's very origins"[3]. The Eucharist is Christ who gives himself to us and continually builds us up as his body. Hence, in the striking interplay between the Eucharist which builds up the Church, and the Church herself which "makes" the Eucharist[4], the primary causality is expressed in the first formula: the Church is able to celebrate and adore the mystery of Christ present in the Eucharist precisely because Christ first gave himself to her in the sacrifice of the Cross. The Church's ability to "make" the Eucharist is completely rooted in Christ's self-gift to her. Here we can see more clearly the meaning of Saint John's words: "he first loved us" (1 Jn 4:19). We too, at every celebration of the Eucharist, confess the primacy of Christ's gift. The causal influence of the Eucharist at the Church's origins definitively discloses both the chronological and ontological priority of the fact that it was Christ who loved us "first." For all eternity he remains the one who loves us first.

The Eucharist is thus constitutive of the Church's being and activity. This is why Christian antiquity used the same words, *Corpus Christi*, to designate Christ's body born of the Virgin Mary, his eucharistic body and his ecclesial body.[5] This clear datum of the tradition helps us to appreciate the inseparability of Christ and the Church. The Lord Jesus, by offering himself in sacrifice for us, in his gift effectively pointed to the mystery of the Church. It is significant that the Second Eucharistic Prayer, invoking the Paraclete, formulates its prayer for the unity of the

Church as follows: *"may all of us who share in the body and blood of Christ be brought together in unity by the Holy Spirit."* These words help us to see clearly how the *res* of the sacrament of the Eucharist is the unity of the faithful within ecclesial communion. The Eucharist is thus found at the root of the Church as a mystery of communion[6].

The mission of the Church

Saint John powerfully expresses the fundamental paradox of the Christian faith. On the one hand, he says that "no one has ever seen God" (Jn 1:18; cf. 1 Jn 4:12). In no way can our imaginations, our concepts or our words ever define or embrace the infinite reality of the Most High. He remains *Deus semper maior*. Yet Saint John also tells us that the Word truly "became flesh" (Jn 1:14). The only-begotten Son, who is ever with the Father, has made known the God whom "no one has ever seen" (Jn 1:18). Jesus Christ comes to us, "full of grace and truth" (Jn 1:14), to give us these gifts (cf. Jn 1:17); and "from his fullness we have all received, grace upon grace" (Jn 1:16). In the Prologue of his Gospel, John thus contemplates the Word from his being with God to his becoming flesh and his return to the Father with our humanity, which he has assumed for ever. In this coming forth from God and returning to him (cf. Jn 13:3; 16:28; 17:8,10), Christ is presented as the one who "tells us" about God (cf. Jn 1:18).

Indeed, as Saint Irenaeus of Lyons says, the Son "is the revealer of the Father".[7] Jesus of Nazareth is, so to speak, the "exegete" of the God whom "no one has ever seen". "He is the image of the invisible God" (Col 1:15). Here we see fulfilled the prophecy of Isaiah about the effectiveness of the Lord's word: as the rain and snow come down from heaven to water and to make the earth fruitful, so too the word of God "shall not return to me empty, but it shall accomplish that which I purpose, and prosper in the thing for which I sent it" (cf. Is 55:10f.). Jesus Christ is this definitive and effective word which came forth from the Father and returned to him, perfectly accomplishing his will in the world.

The word of God has bestowed upon us the divine life which transfigures the face of the earth, making all things new (cf. Rev 21:5). His word engages us not only as *hearers* of divine revelation, but also as its *heralds*. The one whom the Father has sent to do his will (cf. Jn 5:36-38; 6:38-40; 7:16-18) draws us to himself and makes us part of his life and mission. The Spirit of the Risen Lord empowers us to proclaim the word everywhere by the witness of our lives. This was experienced by the first Christian community, which saw the word spread through preaching and witness (cf. Acts 6:7). Here we can think in particular of the life of the Apostle Paul, a man completely caught up by the Lord (cf. Phil 3:12) – "it is no longer I who live, but Christ who lives in me" (Gal 2:20) – and by his mission: "woe to me if I do not proclaim the Gospel!" (1 Cor 9:16). Paul knew well that what was revealed in Christ is really salvation for all peoples, liberation from the slavery of sin in order to enjoy the freedom of the children of God.

What the Church proclaims to the world is the *Logos of Hope* (cf. 1 Pet 3:15); in order to be able to live fully each moment, men and women need "the great hope" which is "the God who possesses a human face and who 'has loved us to the end' (Jn 13:1)".[8] This is why the Church is missionary by her very nature. We cannot keep to ourselves the words of eternal life given to us in our encounter with Jesus Christ: they are meant for everyone, for every man and woman. Everyone today, whether he or she knows it or not, needs this message. May the Lord himself, as in the time of the prophet Amos, raise up in our midst a new hunger and thirst for the word of God (cf. Amos 8:11). It is our responsibility to pass on what, by God's grace, we ourselves have received.

The Synod of Bishops forcefully reaffirmed the need within the Church for a revival of the missionary consciousness present in the People of God from the beginning. The first Christians saw their missionary preaching as a necessity rooted in the very nature of faith: the God in whom they believed was the God of all, the one true God who revealed himself in Israel's history and ultimately in his Son, who thus provided the response which, in their inmost being, all men and women awaited. The first Christian communities felt that their faith was not part of a particular cultural tradition, differing from one people to another, but belonged instead to the realm of truth, which concerns everyone equally.

Once more it is Saint Paul who, by his life, illustrates the meaning of the Christian mission and its fundamental universality. We can think here of the episode related in the Acts of the Apostles about the Athenian Areopagus (cf. 17:16-34). The Apostle of the Nations enters into dialogue with people of various cultures precisely because he is conscious that the mystery of God, Known yet Unknown, which every man and woman perceives, however confusedly, has really been revealed in history: "What therefore you worship as unknown, this I proclaim to you" (Acts 17:23). In fact, the newness of Christian proclamation is that we can tell all peoples: "God has shown himself. In person. And now the way to him is open. The novelty of the Christian message does not consist in an idea but in a fact: God has revealed himself".[9]

Consequently, the Church's mission cannot be considered as an optional or supplementary element in her life. Rather it entails letting the Holy Spirit assimilate us to Christ himself, and thus to share in his own mission: "As the Father has sent me, so I send you" (Jn 20:21) to share the word with your entire life. It is the word itself which impels us towards our brothers and sisters: it is the word which illuminates, purifies, converts; we are only its servants.

We need, then, to discover ever anew the urgency and the beauty of the proclamation of the word for the coming of the Kingdom of God which Christ himself preached. Thus we grow in the realization, so clear to the Fathers of the Church, that the proclamation of the word has as its content the Kingdom of God (cf. Mk 1:14-15), which, in the memorable phrase of Origen,[10] *is the very person of Jesus (Autobasileia)*. The Lord offers salvation to men and women in every age. All of us recognize how much the light of Christ needs to illumine every area of human life: the family, schools, culture, work, leisure and the other aspects of social life.[11] It is not a matter of preaching a word of consolation, but rather a word which disrupts, which calls to conversion and which opens the way to an encounter with the one through whom a new humanity flowers.

Since the entire People of God is a people which has been "sent", the Synod reaffirmed that "the mission of proclaiming the word of God is the task of all of the disciples of Jesus Christ based on their Baptism".[12] No believer in Christ can feel dispensed from this responsibility which comes from the fact of our sacramentally belonging to the Body of Christ. A consciousness of this must be revived in every family, parish, community, association and ecclesial movement. The Church, as a mystery of communion, is thus entirely missionary, and everyone, according to his or her proper state in life, is called to give an incisive contribution to the proclamation of Christ.

Bishops and priests, in accordance with their specific mission, are the first to be called to live a life completely at the service of the word, to proclaim the Gospel, to celebrate the sacraments and to form the faithful in the authentic knowledge of Scripture. Deacons too must feel themselves called to cooperate, in accordance with their specific mission, in this task of evangelization.

Throughout the Church's history the consecrated life has been outstanding for explicitly taking up the task of proclaiming and preaching the word of God in the *missio ad gentes* and in the most difficult situations, for being ever ready to adapt to new situations and for setting out courageously and boldly along fresh paths in meeting new challenges for the effective proclamation of God's word.[13]

The laity are called to exercise their own prophetic role, which derives directly from their Baptism, and to bear witness to the Gospel in daily life, wherever they find themselves. In this regard the Synod Fathers expressed "the greatest esteem, gratitude and encouragement for the service to evangelization which so many of the lay faithful, and women in particular, provide with generosity and commitment in their communities throughout the world, following the example of Mary Magdalene, the first witness of the joy of Easter".[14] The Synod also recognized with gratitude that the ecclesial movements and the new communities are a great force for evangelization in our times and an incentive to the development of new ways of proclaiming the Gospel.[15]

In calling upon all the faithful to proclaim God's word, the Synod Fathers restated the need in our day too for a decisive commitment to the *missio ad gentes*. In no way can the Church restrict her pastoral work to the "ordinary maintenance" of those who already know the Gospel of Christ. Missionary outreach is a clear sign of the maturity of an ecclesial community. The Fathers also insisted that the word of God is the saving truth which men and women in every age need to hear. For this reason, it must be explicitly proclaimed. The Church must go out to meet each person in the strength of the Spirit (cf. 1 Cor 2:5) and continue her prophetic defence of people's right and freedom to hear the word of God, while constantly seeking out the most effective ways of proclaiming that word, even at the risk of persecution.[16] The Church feels duty-bound to proclaim to every man and woman the word that saves (cf. Rom 1:14).

Endnotes

1. Cf. Second Vatican Ecumenical Council, Dogmatic Constitution on the Church *Lumen Gentium*, 3; for an example, see: Saint John Chrysostom, *Catechesis* 3, 13-19: SC 50, 174-177.

2. John Paul II, Encyclical Letter *Ecclesia de Eucharistia* (17 April 2003), 1: AAS 95 (2003), 433.

3. *Ibid.*, 21: AAS 95 (2003), 447.

4. Cf. John Paul II, Encyclical Letter *Redemptor Hominis* (4 March 1979), 20: AAS 71 (1979), 309-316; Apostolic Letter *Dominicae Cenae* (24 February 1980), 4: AAS 72 (1980), 119-121.

5. Cf. *Propositio* 5.

6. Cf. Saint Thomas Aquinas, *Summa Theologiae*, III, q. 80, a. 4.

7. *Adversus Haereses*, IV, 20, 7: PG 7, 1037.

8. Benedict XVI, Encyclical Letter *Spe Salvi* (30 November 2007), 31: AAS 99 (2007), 1010.

9. Benedict XVI, *Address to Representatives of the World of Culture at the "Collège des Bernardins" in Paris* (12 September 2008): AAS 100 (2008), 730.

10. Cf. *In Evangelium secundum Matthaeum* 17:7: PG 13, 1197B; Saint Jerome, *Translatio homiliarum Origenis in Lucam*, 36: PL 26, 324-325.

11. Cf. Benedict XVI, *Homily for the Opening of the Twelfth Ordinary General Assembly of the Synod of Bishops* (5 October 2008): AAS 100 (2008), 757.

12. *Propositio* 38.

13. Cf. Congregation for Institutes of consecrated life and for societies of apostolic life, Instruction *Starting Afresh from Christ: A Renewed Commitment to Consecrated Life in the Third Millennium* (19 May 2002), 36: *Enchiridion Vaticanum* 21, Nos. 488-491.

14. *Propositio* 30.

15. Cf. *Propositio* 38.

16. Cf. *Propositio* 49.

VIRGIN MARY

Full of grace

In the Incarnation of the Son of God, in fact, we recognize the origins of the Church. Everything began from there. Every historical realization of the Church and every one of her institutions must be shaped by that primordial wellspring. They must be shaped by Christ, the incarnate Word of God. It is he that we are constantly celebrating: Emmanuel, God-with-us, through whom the saving will of God the Father has been accomplished. And yet – today of all days we contemplate this aspect of the Mystery – the divine wellspring flows through a privileged channel: the Virgin Mary. St Bernard speaks of this using the eloquent image of *aquaeductus* (cf. *Sermo in Nativitate B.V. Mariae: PL* 183, 437-448). In celebrating the Incarnation of the Son, therefore, we cannot fail to honour his Mother. The Angel's proclamation was addressed to her; she accepted it, and when she responded from the depths of her heart: "Here I am... let it be done to me according to your word" (Lk 1:38), at that moment the eternal Word began to exist as a human being in time.

From generation to generation, the wonder evoked by this ineffable mystery never ceases. St Augustine imagines a dialogue between himself and the Angel of the Annunciation, in which he asks: "Tell me, O Angel, why did this happen in Mary?". The answer, says the Messenger, is contained in the very words of the greeting: "Hail, full of grace" (cf. *Sermo* 291: 6). In fact, the Angel, "appearing to her", does not call her by her earthly name, Mary, but by her divine name, as she has always been seen and characterized by God: "Full of grace - *gratia plena*", which in the original Greek is κεχαριτωμένη, "full of grace", and the grace is none other than the love of God; thus, in the end, we can translate this word: "beloved" of God (cf. Lk 1:28). Origen observes that no such title had ever been given to a human being, and that it is unparalleled in all of Sacred Scripture (cf. *In Lucam* 6: 7). It is a title expressed in passive form, but this "passivity" of Mary, who has always been and is for ever "loved" by the Lord, implies her free consent, her personal and original response: in *being loved*, in receiving the gift of God, Mary is fully *active*, because she accepts with personal generosity the wave of God's love poured out upon her. In this too, she is the perfect disciple of her Son, who realizes the fullness of his freedom and thus exercises the freedom through obedience to the Father. In the Second Reading, we heard the wonderful passage in which the author of the Letter to the Hebrews interprets Psalm 39 in the light of Christ's Incarnation: "When Christ came into the world, he said: ..."Here I am, I have come to do your will, O God'" (Heb 10:5-7). Before the mystery of these two "Here I am" statements, the "Here I am" of the Son and the "Here I am" of the Mother, each of which is reflected in the other, forming a single *Amen* to God's loving will, we are filled with wonder and thanksgiving, and we bow down in adoration.

What a great gift, dear Brothers, to be able to conduct this evocative celebration on the Solemnity of the Lord's Annunciation! What an abundance of light we can draw from this mystery for our lives as ministers of the Church! You above all, dear new Cardinals, what great sustenance you can receive for your mission as the eminent "Senate" of Peter's Successor! This providential circumstance helps us to consider today's event, which emphasizes the *Petrine* principle of the Church, in the light of the other principle, the *Marian* one, which is even more fundamental. The importance of the Marian principle in the Church was particularly highlighted, after the Council, by my beloved Predecessor Pope John Paul II in harmony with his motto *Totus tuus*. In his spirituality and in his tireless ministry, the presence of Mary as Mother and Queen of the Church was made manifest to the eyes of all. More than ever he adverted to her maternal presence in the assassination attempt of 13 May 1981 here in St Peter's Square. In memory of that tragic event, he had a mosaic of the Virgin placed high up in the Apostolic Palace looking down over St Peter's Square, so as to accompany the key moments and the daily unfolding of his long reign. It is just one year since his Pontificate entered its final phase, full of suffering and yet triumphant and truly paschal. The icon of the Annunciation, more than any other, helps us to see clearly how everything in the Church goes back to that mystery of Mary's acceptance of the divine Word, by which, through the action of the Holy Spirit, the Covenant between God and humanity was perfectly sealed. Everything in the Church, every institution and ministry, including that of Peter and his Successors, is "included" under the Virgin's mantle, within the grace-filled horizon of her "yes" to God's will. This link with Mary naturally evokes a strong affective resonance in all of us, but first of all it has an objective value. Between Mary and the Church there is indeed a connatural relationship that was strongly emphasized by the Second Vatican Council in its felicitous decision to place the treatment of the Blessed Virgin at the conclusion of the Constitution on the Church, *Lumen Gentium*. […]

The two dimensions of the Church, Marian and Petrine, come together in the supreme value of *charity*, which constitutes the fulfillment of each. As St Paul says, charity is the "greatest" charism, the "most excellent way" (1 Cor 12:31; 13:13).

Everything in this world will pass away. In eternity only Love will remain. For this reason, my Brothers, taking the opportunity offered by this favourable time of Lent, let us commit ourselves to ensure that everything in our personal lives and in the ecclesial activity in which we are engaged is inspired by charity and leads to charity. In this respect too, we are enlightened by the mystery that we are celebrating today. Indeed, the first thing that Mary did after receiving the Angel's message was to go "in haste" to the house of her cousin Elizabeth in order to be of service to her (cf. Lk 1:39). The Virgin's initiative was one of genuine charity; it was humble and courageous, motivated by faith in God's Word and the inner promptings of the Holy Spirit. Those who love forget about themselves and place themselves at the service of their neighbour. Here we have the image and model of the Church! Every Ecclesial Community, like the Mother of Christ, is called to accept with total generosity the mystery of God who comes to dwell within her and guides her steps in the ways of love. This is the path along which I chose to launch my Pontificate, inviting everyone, with my first Encyclical, to build up the Church in charity as a "community of love" (cf . *Deus Caritas Est*, Part II).

Mother of God

"Mother of God", *Theotokos,* is the title that was officially attributed to Mary in the fifth century, to be exact, at the Council of Ephesus in 431, but which had already taken root in the devotion of the Christian people since the third century, in the context of the heated discussions on the Person of Christ in that period. This title highlights the fact that Christ is God and truly was born of Mary as a man: in this way his unity as true God and true man is preserved. Actually, however much the debate might seem to focus on Mary, it essentially concerned the Son. Desiring to safeguard the full humanity of Jesus, several Fathers suggested a weaker term: instead of the title *Theotokos,* they suggested *Christotokos,* "Mother of Christ"; however, this was rightly seen as a threat to the doctrine of the full unity of Christ's divinity with his humanity. On the one hand, therefore, after lengthy discussion at the Council of Ephesus in 431, as I said, the unity of the two natures – the divine and the human (cf. *DS*, n. 250) – in the Person of the Son of God was solemnly confirmed and, on the other, the legitimacy of the attribution of the title *Theotokos,* Mother of God, to the Virgin (*ibid.*, n. 251).

After this Council a true explosion of Marian devotion was recorded and many churches dedicated to the Mother of God were built. Outstanding among these is the Basilica of St Mary Major here in Rome. The teaching on Mary, Mother of God, received further confirmation at the Council of Chalcedon (451), at which Christ was declared "true God and true man... born for us and for our salvation of Mary, Virgin and Mother of God, in his humanity" (*DS*, n. 301). As is well known, the Second Vatican Council gathered the teachings on Mary in the eighth chapter of the Dogmatic Constitution on the Church Lumen Gentium, reaffirming her divine motherhood. The chapter is entitled "The Blessed Virgin Mary, Mother of God, in the Mystery of Christ and the Church".

Thus, the description "Mother of God", so deeply bound up with the Christmas festivities, is therefore the fundamental name with which the Community of Believers has always honoured the Blessed Virgin. It clearly explains Mary's mission in salvation history. All other titles attributed to Our Lady are based on her vocation to be the Mother of the Redeemer, the human creature chosen by God to bring about the plan of salvation, centred on the great mystery of the Incarnation of the Divine Word. In these days of festivity we have paused to contemplate the depiction of the Nativity in the crib. At the centre of this scene we find the Virgin Mother, who offers the Baby Jesus for the contemplation of all those who come to adore the Saviour: the shepherds, the poor people of Bethlehem, the Magi from the East. Later, on the Feast of the "Presentation" which we celebrate on 2 February, it will be the elderly Simeon and the prophetess Anna who receive the tiny Infant from the hands of his Mother and worship him. The devotion of the Christian people has always considered the Birth of Jesus and the divine motherhood of Mary as two aspects of the same mystery of the Incarnation of the Divine Word, so it has never thought of the Nativity as a thing of the past. We are "contemporaries" of the shepherds, the Magi, of Simeon and of Anna, and as we go with them we are filled with joy, because God wanted to be the God-with-us and has a mother who is our mother.

All the other titles with which the Church honours Our Lady then derive from the title "Mother of God", but this one is fundamental. Let us think of the privilege of the "Immaculate Conception", that is, of Mary being immune to sin from conception: she was preserved from any stain of sin because she was to be the Mother of the Redeemer. The same applies to the title "Our Lady of the Assumption": the One who had brought forth the Saviour could not be subject to the corruption that derives from original sin. And we know that all these privileges were not granted in order to distance Mary from us but, on the contrary, to bring her close; indeed, since she was totally with God, this woman is very close to us and helps us as a mother and a sister. The unique and unrepeatable position that Mary occupies in the Community of Believers also stems from her fundamental vocation to being Mother of the Redeemer. Precisely as such, Mary is also Mother of the Mystical Body of Christ, which is the Church. Rightly, therefore, on 21 November 1964 during the Second Vatican Council, Paul VI solemnly attributed to Mary the title "Mother of the Church".

It is because she is Mother of the Church that the Virgin is also the Mother of each one of us, members of the Mystical Body of Christ. From the Cross, Jesus entrusted his Mother to all his disciples and at the same time entrusted all his disciples to the love of his Mother. The Evangelist John concludes the brief and evocative account with these words: "Then he said to the disciple, "Behold, your mother!'. And from that hour the disciple took her to his own home" (Jn 19:27). This is the [English] translation of the Greek text "εἰς τά ἴδια", he welcomed her into his own reality, his own existence. Thus, she is part of his life and the two lives penetrate each other. And this acceptance of her (εἰς τά ἴδια) in his own life is the Lord's testament. Therefore, at the supreme moment of the fulfilment of his messianic mission, Jesus bequeathes as a precious inheritance to each one of his disciples his own Mother, the Virgin Mary

Mother of the Church

Pope Paul VI solemnly concluded the Second Vatican Council in the square in front of St Peter's Basilica forty years ago, on 8 December 1965. It had been inaugurated, in accordance with John XXIII's wishes, on 11 October 1962, which was then the Feast of Mary's Motherhood, and ended on the day of the Immaculate Conception. The Council took place in a Marian setting. It was actually far more than a setting: it was the orientation of its entire process. It refers us, as it referred the Council Fathers at that time, to the image of the Virgin who listens and lives in the Word of God, who cherishes in her heart the words that God addresses to her and, piecing them together like a mosaic, learns to understand them (cf. Lk 2:19,51). It refers us to the great Believer who, full of faith, put herself in God's hands, abandoning herself to his will; it refers us to the humble Mother who, when the Son's mission so required, became part of it, and at the same time, to the courageous woman who stood beneath the Cross while the disciples fled. In his Discourse on the occasion of the promulgation of the Dogmatic Constitution on the Church, Paul VI described Mary as *"tutrix huius Concilii"*, "Patroness of this Council*"*, (cf. *Oecumenicum Concilium Vaticanum II, Constitutiones Decreta Declarationes,* Vatican City, 1966, p. 983) and, with an unmistakable allusion to the account of Pentecost transmitted by Luke (cf. Acts 1:12-14), said that the Fathers were gathered in the Council Hall *"cum Maria, Matre Iesu"* and would also have left it in her name (p. 985).

Indelibly printed in my memory is the moment when, hearing his words: *"Mariam Sanctissimam declaramus Matrem Ecclesiae"* – "We declare Mary the Most Holy Mother of the Church", the Fathers spontaneously rose at once and paid homage to the Mother of God, to our Mother, to the Mother of the Church, with a standing ovation. Indeed, with this title the Pope summed up the Marian teaching of the Council and provided the key to understanding it. Not only does Mary have a unique relationship with Christ, the Son of God who, as man, chose to become her Son. Since she was totally united to Christ, she also totally belongs to us. Yes, we can say that Mary is close to us as no other human being is, because Christ becomes man for all men and women and his entire being is "being here for us". Christ, the Fathers said, as the Head, is inseparable from his Body which is the Church, forming with her, so to speak, a single living subject. The Mother of the Head is also the Mother of all the Church; she is, so to speak, totally emptied of herself; she has given herself entirely to Christ and with him is given as a gift to us all. Indeed, the more the human person gives himself, the more he finds himself.

The Council intended to tell us this: Mary is so interwoven in the great mystery of the Church that she and the Church are inseparable, just as she and Christ are inseparable. Mary mirrors the Church, anticipates the Church in her person, and in all the turbulence that affects the suffering, struggling Church she always remains the Star of salvation. In her lies the true centre in which we trust, even if its peripheries very often weigh on our soul. In the context of the promulgation of the Constitution on the Church, Paul VI shed light on all this through a new title deeply rooted in Tradition, precisely with the intention of illuminating the inner structure of the Church's teaching, which was developed at the Council. The Second Vatican Council had to pronounce on the institutional components of the Church: on the Bishops and on the Pontiff, on the priests, lay people and Religious, in their communion and in their relations; it had to describe the Church journeying on, "clasping sinners to her bosom, at once holy and always in need of purification..." (*Lumen Gentium*, n. 8). This "Petrine" aspect of the Church, however, is included in that "Marian" aspect. In Mary, the Immaculate, we find the essence of the Church without distortion. We ourselves must learn from her to become "ecclesial souls", as the Fathers said, so that we too may be able, in accordance with St Paul's words, to present ourselves "blameless" in the sight of the Lord, as he wanted us from the very beginning (cf. Col 1:21; Eph 1:4).

But now we must ask ourselves: What does "Mary, the Immaculate" mean? Does this title have something to tell us? Today, the liturgy illuminates the content of these words for us in two great images. First of all comes the marvellous narrative of the annunciation of the Messiah's coming to Mary, the Virgin of Nazareth. The Angel's greeting is interwoven with threads from the Old Testament, especially from the Prophet Zephaniah. He shows that Mary, the humble provincial woman who comes from a priestly race and bears within her the great priestly patrimony of Israel, is "the holy remnant" of Israel to which the prophets referred in all the periods of trial and darkness. In her is present the true Zion, the pure, living dwelling-place of God. In her the Lord dwells, in her he finds the place of his repose. She is the living house of God, who does not dwell in buildings of stone but in the heart of living man. She is the shoot which sprouts from the stump of David in the dark winter night of history. In her, the words of the Psalm are fulfilled: *"The earth has yielded its fruits"* (Ps 67:7). She is the offshoot from which grew the tree of redemption and of the redeemed. God has not failed, as it might have seemed formerly at the beginning of history with Adam and Eve or during the period of the Babylonian Exile, and as it seemed anew in Mary's time when Israel had become a people with no importance in an occupied region and with very few recognizable signs of its holiness. God did not fail. In the humility of the house in Nazareth lived holy Israel, the pure remnant. God saved and saves his people. From the felled tree trunk Israel's history shone out anew, becoming a living force that guides and pervades the world. Mary is holy Israel: she says "yes" to the Lord, she puts herself totally at his disposal and thus becomes the living temple of God.

The second image is much more difficult and obscure. This metaphor from the Book of Genesis speaks to us from a great historical distance and can only be explained with difficulty; only in the course of history has it been possible to develop a deeper understanding of what it refers to. It was foretold that the struggle between humanity and the serpent, that is, between man and the forces of evil and death, would continue throughout history. It was also foretold, however, that the "offspring" of a woman would one day triumph and would crush the head of the serpent to death; it was foretold that the offspring of the woman – and in this offspring the woman and the mother herself – would be victorious and that thus, through man, God would triumph. If we set ourselves with the believing and praying Church to listen to this text, then we can begin to understand what original sin, inherited sin, is and also what the protection against this inherited sin is, what redemption is.

What picture does this passage show us? The human being does not trust God. Tempted by the serpent, he harbours the suspicion that in the end, God takes something away from his life, that God is a rival who curtails our freedom and that we will be fully human only when we have cast him aside; in brief, that only in this way can we fully achieve our freedom. The human being lives in the suspicion that God's love creates a dependence and that he must rid himself of this dependency if he is to be fully himself. Man does not want to receive his existence and the fullness of his life from God. He himself wants to obtain from the tree of knowledge the power to shape the world, to make himself a god, raising himself to God's level, and to overcome death and darkness with his own efforts. He does not want to rely on love that to him seems untrustworthy; he relies solely on his own knowledge since it confers power upon him. Rather than on love, he sets his sights on power, with which he desires to take his own life autonomously in hand. And in doing so, he trusts in deceit rather than in truth and thereby sinks with his life into emptiness, into death. Love is not dependence but a gift that makes us live. The freedom of a human being is the freedom of a limited being, and therefore is itself limited. We can possess it only as a shared freedom, in the communion of freedom: only if we live in the right way, with one another and for one another, can freedom develop. We live in the right way if we live in accordance with the truth of our being, and that is, in accordance with God's will. For God's will is not a law for the human being imposed from the outside and that constrains him, but the intrinsic measure of his nature, a measure that is engraved within him and makes him the image of God, hence, a free creature. If we live in opposition to love and against the truth – in opposition to God – then we destroy one another and destroy the world. Then we do not find life but act in the interests of death. All this is recounted with immortal images in the history of the original fall of man and the expulsion of man from the earthly Paradise.

If we sincerely reflect about ourselves and our history, we have to say that with this narrative is described not only the history of the beginning but the history of all times, and that we all carry within us a drop of the poison of that way of thinking, illustrated by the images in the Book of Genesis. We call this drop of poison "original sin". Precisely on the Feast of the Immaculate Conception, we have a lurking suspicion that a person who does not sin must really be basically boring and that something is missing from his life: the dramatic dimension of being autonomous; that the freedom to say no, to descend into the shadows of sin and to want to do things on one's own is part of being truly human; that only then can we make the most of all the vastness and depth of our being men and women, of being truly ourselves; that we should put this freedom to the test, even in opposition to God, in order to become, in reality, fully ourselves. In a word, we think that evil is basically good, we think that we need it, at least a little, in order to experience the fullness of being. We think that Mephistopheles – the tempter – is right when he says he is the power "that always wants evil and always does good" (J.W. von Goethe, *Faust* I, 3). We think that a little bargaining with evil, keeping for oneself a little freedom against God, is basically a good thing, perhaps even necessary.

If we look, however, at the world that surrounds us we can see that this is not so; in other words, that evil is always poisonous, does not uplift human beings but degrades and humiliates them. It does not make them any the greater, purer or wealthier, but harms and belittles them. This is something we should indeed learn on the day of the Immaculate Conception: the person who abandons himself totally in God's hands does not become God's puppet, a boring "yes man"; he does not lose his freedom. Only the person who entrusts himself totally to God finds true freedom, the great, creative immensity of the freedom of good. The person who turns to God does not become smaller but greater, for through God and with God he becomes great, he becomes divine, he becomes truly himself. The person who puts himself in God's hands does not distance himself from others, withdrawing into his private salvation; on the contrary, it is only then that his heart truly awakens and he becomes a sensitive, hence, benevolent and open person.

The closer a person is to God, the closer he is to people. We see this in Mary. The fact that she is totally with God is the reason why she is so close to human beings. For this reason she can be the Mother of every consolation and every help, a Mother whom anyone can dare to address in any kind of need in weakness and in sin, for she has understanding for everything and is for everyone the open power of creative goodness. In her, God has impressed his own image, the image of the One who follows the lost sheep even up into the mountains and among the briars and thornbushes of the sins of this world, letting himself be spiked by the crown of thorns of these sins in order to take the sheep on his shoulders and bring it home. As a merciful Mother, Mary is the anticipated figure and everlasting portrait of the Son. Thus, we see that the image of the Sorrowful Virgin, of the Mother who shares her suffering and her love, is also a true image of the Immaculate Conception. Her heart was enlarged by being and feeling together with God. In her, God's goodness came very close to us. Mary thus stands before us as a sign of comfort, encouragement and hope. She turns to us, saying: "Have the courage to dare with God! Try it! Do not be afraid of him! Have the courage to risk with faith! Have the courage to risk with goodness! Have the courage to risk with a pure heart! Commit yourselves to God, then you will see that it is precisely by doing so that your life will become broad and light, not boring but filled with infinite surprises, for God's infinite goodness is never depleted!".

Mother of hope

With a hymn composed in the eighth or ninth century, thus for over a thousand years, the Church has greeted Mary, the Mother of God, as "Star of the Sea": *Ave maris stella*. Human life is a journey. Towards what destination? How do we find the way? Life is like a voyage on the sea of history, often dark and stormy, a voyage in which we watch for the stars that indicate the route. The true stars of our life are the people who have lived good lives. They are lights of hope. Certainly, Jesus Christ is the true light, the sun that has risen above all the shadows of history. But to reach him we also need lights close by – people who shine with his light and so guide us along our way. Who more than Mary could be a star of hope for us? With her "yes" she opened the door of our world to God himself; she became the living Ark of the Covenant, in whom God took flesh, became one of us, and pitched his tent among us (cf. Jn 1:14).

So we cry to her: Holy Mary, you belonged to the humble and great souls of Israel who, like Simeon, were "looking for the consolation of Israel" (Lk 2:25) and hoping, like Anna, "for the redemption of Jerusalem" (Lk 2:38). Your life was thoroughly imbued with the sacred scriptures of Israel which spoke of hope, of the promise made to Abraham and his descendants (cf. Lk 1:55). In this way we can appreciate the holy fear that overcame you when the angel of the Lord appeared to you and told you that you would give birth to the One who was the hope of Israel, the One awaited by the world. Through you, through your "yes", the hope of the ages became reality, entering this world and its history. You bowed low before the greatness of this task and gave your consent: "Behold, I am the handmaid of the Lord; let it be to me according to your word" (Lk 1:38). When you hastened with holy joy across the mountains of Judea to see your cousin Elizabeth, you became the image of the Church to come, which carries the hope of the world in her womb across the mountains of history. But alongside the joy which, with your *Magnificat,* you proclaimed in word and song for all the centuries to hear, you also knew the dark sayings of the prophets about the suffering of the servant of God in this world. Shining over his birth in the stable at Bethlehem, there were angels in splendour who brought the good news to the shepherds, but at the same time the lowliness of God in this world was all too palpable. The old man Simeon spoke to you of the sword which would pierce your soul (cf. Lk 2:35), of the sign of contradiction that your Son would be in this world. Then, when Jesus began his public ministry, you had to step aside, so that a new family could grow, the family which it was his mission to establish and which would be made up of those who heard his word and kept it (cf. Lk 11:27f). Notwithstanding the great joy that marked the beginning of Jesus's ministry, in the synagogue of Nazareth you must already have experienced the truth of the saying about the "sign of contradiction" (cf. Lk 4:28ff). In this way you saw the growing power of hostility and rejection which built up around Jesus until the hour of the Cross, when you had to look upon the Saviour of the world, the heir of David, the Son of God dying like a failure, exposed to mockery, between criminals. Then you received the word of Jesus: "Woman, behold, your Son!" (Jn 19:26). From the Cross you received a new mission. From the Cross you became a mother in a new way: the mother of all those who believe in your Son Jesus and wish to follow him. The sword of sorrow pierced your heart. Did hope die? Did the world remain definitively without light, and life without purpose? At that moment, deep down, you probably listened again to the word spoken by the angel in answer to your fear at the time of the Annunciation: "Do not be afraid, Mary!" (Lk 1:30). How many times had the Lord, your Son, said the same thing to his disciples: do not be afraid! In your heart, you heard this word again during the night of Golgotha. Before the hour of his betrayal he had said to his disciples: "Be of good cheer, I have overcome the world" (Jn 16:33). "Let not your hearts be troubled, neither let them be afraid" (Jn 14:27). "Do not be afraid, Mary!" In that hour at Nazareth the angel had also said to you: "Of his kingdom there will be no end" (Lk 1:33). Could it have ended before it began? No, at the foot of the Cross, on the strength of Jesus's own word, you became the mother of believers. In this faith, which even in the darkness of Holy Saturday bore the certitude of hope, you made your way towards Easter morning. The joy of the Resurrection touched your heart and united you in a new way to the disciples, destined to become the family of Jesus through faith. In this way you were in the midst of the community of believers, who in the days following the Ascension prayed with one voice for the gift of the Holy Spirit (cf. Acts 1:14) and then received that gift on the day of Pentecost. The "Kingdom" of Jesus was not as might have been imagined. It began in that hour, and of this "Kingdom" there will be no end. Thus you remain in the midst of the disciples as their Mother, as the Mother of hope. Holy Mary, Mother of God, our Mother, teach us to believe, to hope, to love with you. Show us the way to his Kingdom! Star of the Sea, shine upon us and guide us on our way!

THE SACRAMENTS

The symbolism of the sacramental signs

At the centre of the Church's worship is the notion of "sacrament". This means that it is not primarily we who act, but God comes first to meet us through his action, he looks upon us and he leads us to himself. Another striking feature is this: God touches us through material things, through gifts of creation that he takes up into his service, making them instruments of the encounter between us and himself. There are four elements in creation on which the world of sacraments is built: water, bread, wine and olive oil. Water, as the basic element and fundamental condition of all life, is the essential sign of the act in which, through baptism, we become Christians and are born to new life. While water is the vital element everywhere, and thus represents the shared access of all people to rebirth as Christians, the other three elements belong to the culture of the Mediterranean region. In other words, they point towards the concrete historical environment in which Christianity emerged. God acted in a clearly defined place on the earth, he truly made history with men. On the one hand, these three elements are gifts of creation, and on the other, they also indicate the locality of the history of God with us. They are a synthesis between creation and history: gifts of God that always connect us to those parts of the world where God chose to act with us in historical time, where he chose to become one of us.

Within these three elements there is a further gradation. Bread has to do with everyday life. It is the fundamental gift of life day by day. Wine has to do with feasting, with the fine things of creation, in which, at the same time, the joy of the redeemed finds particular expression. Olive oil has a wide range of meaning. It is nourishment, it is medicine, it gives beauty, it prepares us for battle and it gives strength. Kings and priests are anointed with oil, which is thus a sign of dignity and responsibility, and likewise of the strength that comes from God. Even the name that we bear as "Christians" contains the mystery of the oil. The word "Christians", in fact, by which Christ's disciples were known in the earliest days of Gentile Christianity, is derived from the word "Christ" (Acts 11:20-21) – the Greek translation of the word "Messiah", which means "anointed one". To be a Christian is to come from Christ, to belong to Christ, to the anointed one of God, to whom God granted kingship and priesthood. It means belonging to him whom God himself anointed – not with material oil, but with the One whom the oil represents: with his Holy Spirit. Olive oil is thus in a very particular way a symbol of the total compenetration of the man Jesus by the Holy Spirit.

In the Chrism Mass on Holy Thursday, the holy oils are at the centre of the liturgical action. They are consecrated in the bishop's cathedral for the whole year. They thus serve also as an expression of the Church's unity, guaranteed by the episcopate, and they point to Christ, the true "shepherd and guardian" of our souls, as Saint Peter calls him (1 Pet 2:25). At the same time, they hold together the entire liturgical year, anchored in the mystery of Holy Thursday. Finally, they point to the Garden of Olives, the scene of Jesus' inner acceptance of his Passion. Yet the Garden of Olives is also the place from which he ascended to the Father, and is therefore the place of redemption: God did not leave Jesus in death. Jesus lives for ever with the Father, and is therefore omnipresent, with us always. This double mystery of the Mount of Olives is also always "at work" within the Church's sacramental oil. In four sacraments, oil is the sign of God's goodness reaching out to touch us: in baptism, in confirmation as the sacrament of the Holy Spirit, in the different grades of the sacrament of holy orders and finally in the anointing of the sick, in which oil is offered to us, so to speak, as God's medicine – as the medicine which now assures us of his goodness, offering us strength and consolation, yet at the same time points beyond the moment of the illness towards the definitive healing, the resurrection (cf. Jas 5:14). Thus oil, in its different forms, accompanies us throughout our lives: beginning with the catechumenate and baptism, and continuing right up to the moment when we prepare to meet God, our Judge and Saviour. Moreover, the Chrism Mass, in which the sacramental sign of oil is presented to us as part of the language of God's creation, speaks in particular to us who are priests: it speaks of Christ, whom God anointed King and Priest – of him who makes us sharers in his priesthood, in his "anointing", through our own priestly ordination.

I should like, then, to attempt a brief interpretation of the mystery of this holy sign in its essential reference to the priestly vocation. In popular etymologies a connection was made, even in ancient times, between the Greek word "*elaion*" – oil – and the word "*eleos*" – mercy. In fact, in the various sacraments, consecrated oil is always a sign of God's mercy. So the meaning of priestly anointing always includes the mission to bring God's mercy to those we serve. In the lamp of our lives, the oil of mercy should never run dry. Let us always obtain it from the Lord in good time – in our encounter with his word, in our reception of the sacraments, in the time we spend with him in prayer.

As a consequence of the story of the dove bearing an olive branch to signal the end of the flood – and thus God's new peace with the world of men – not only the dove but also the olive branch and oil itself have become symbols of peace. The Christians of antiquity loved to decorate the tombs of their dead with the crown of victory and the olive branch, symbol of peace. They knew that Christ conquered death and that their dead were resting in the peace of Christ. They knew that they themselves were awaited by Christ, that he had promised them the peace which the world cannot give. They remembered that the first words of the Risen Lord to his disciples were: "Peace be with you!" (Jn 20:19). He himself, so to speak, bears the olive branch, he introduces his peace into the world. He announces God's saving goodness. He is our peace. Christians should therefore be people of peace, people who recognize and live the mystery of the Cross as a mystery of reconciliation. Christ does not conquer through the sword, but through the Cross. He wins by conquering hatred. He wins through the force of his greater love. The Cross of Christ expresses his "no" to violence. And in this way, it is God's victory sign, which announces Jesus' new way. The one who suffered was stronger than the ones who exercised power. In his self-giving on the Cross, Christ conquered violence. As priests we are called, in fellowship with Jesus Christ, to be men of peace, we are called to oppose violence and to trust in the greater power of love.

A further aspect of the symbolism of oil is that it strengthens for battle. This does not contradict the theme of peace, but forms part of it. The battle of Christians consisted – and still consists – not in the use of violence, but in the fact that they were – and are – ready to suffer for the good, for God. It consists in the fact that Christians, as good citizens, keep the law and do what is just and good. It consists in the fact that they do not do whatever within the legal system in force is not just but unjust. The battle of the martyrs consists in their concrete "no" to injustice: by taking no part in idolatry, in Emperor worship, they refused to bow down before falsehood, before the adoration of human persons and their power. With their "no" to falsehood and all its consequences, they upheld the power of right and truth. Thus they served true peace. Today too it is important for Christians to follow what is right, which is the foundation of peace. Today too it is important for Christians not to accept a wrong that is enshrined in law – for example the killing of innocent unborn children. In this way we serve peace, in this way we find ourselves following in the footsteps of Jesus Christ, of whom Saint Peter says: "When he was reviled he did not revile in return; when he suffered, he did not threaten; but he trusted to him who judges justly. He himself bore our sins in his body on the tree, that we might die to sin and live to righteousness" (1 Pet 2:23f.).

The beginning of the journey in the Christian life

How can we allow ourselves to be renewed by the Holy Spirit and to grow in our spiritual lives? The answer, as you know, is this: we can do so by means of the Sacraments, because faith is born and is strengthened within us through the Sacraments, particularly those of Christian initiation: Baptism, Confirmation and the Eucharist, which are complementary and inseparable (cf. *The Catechism of the Catholic Church*, 1285). This truth concerning the three Sacraments that initiate our lives as Christians is perhaps neglected in the faith life of many Christians. They view them as events that took place in the past and have no real significance for today, like roots that lack life-giving nourishment. It happens that many young people distance themselves from their life of faith after they have received Confirmation. There are also young people who have not even received this sacrament. Yet it is through the sacraments of Baptism, Confirmation and then, in an ongoing way, the Eucharist, that the Holy Spirit makes us children of the Father, brothers and sisters of Jesus, members of his Church, capable of a true witness to the Gospel, and able to savour the joy of faith.

I therefore invite you to reflect on what I am writing to you. Nowadays it is particularly necessary to rediscover the sacrament of Confirmation and its important place in our spiritual growth. Those who have received the sacraments of Baptism and Confirmation should remember that they have become "temples of the Spirit": God lives within them. Always be aware of this and strive to allow the treasure within you to bring forth fruits of holiness. Those who are baptized but have not yet received the sacrament of Confirmation, prepare to receive it knowing that in this way you will become "complete" Christians, since Confirmation perfects baptismal grace (cf. *The Catechism of the Catholic Church*, 1302-1304).

Confirmation gives us *special strength* to witness to and glorify God with our whole lives (cf. Rom 12:1). It makes us intimately aware of our belonging to the Church, the "Body of Christ", of which we are all living members, in solidarity with one another (cf. 1 Cor 12:12-25). By allowing themselves to be guided by the Spirit, each baptized person can bring his or her own contribution to the building up of the Church because of the *charisms* given by the Spirit, for "to *each* is given the manifestation of the Spirit for the *common good*" (1 Cor 12:7). When the Spirit acts, he brings his fruits to the soul, namely "love, joy, peace, patience, kindness, generosity, faithfulness, gentleness, and self-control" (Gal 5:22). To those of you who have not yet received the sacrament of Confirmation, I extend a cordial invitation to prepare to receive it, and to seek help from your priests. It is a special occasion of grace that the Lord is offering you. Do not miss this opportunity!

I would like to add a word about the Eucharist. In order to grow in our Christian life, we need to be nourished by the Body and Blood of Christ. In fact, we are baptized and confirmed with a view to the Eucharist (cf. *The Catechism of the Catholic Church*, 1322; *Sacramentum Caritatis*, 17). "Source and summit" of the Church's life, the Eucharist is a "perpetual Pentecost" since every time we celebrate Mass we receive the Holy Spirit who unites us more deeply with Christ and transforms us into Him. My dear young friends, if you take part frequently in the eucharistic celebration, if you dedicate some of your time to adoration of the Blessed Sacrament, the Source of love which is the Eucharist, you will acquire that joyful determination to dedicate your lives to following the Gospel. At the same time it will be your experience that whenever our strength is not enough, it is the Holy Spirit who transforms us, filling us with his strength and making us witnesses suffused by the missionary fervour of the risen Christ.

The gift of a new identity

In his farewell discourse, Jesus announced his imminent death and resurrection to his disciples with these mysterious words: "I go away, and I will come to you", he said (Jn 14:28). Dying is a "going away". Even if the body of the deceased remains behind, he himself has gone away into the unknown, and we cannot follow him (cf. Jn 13:36). Yet in Jesus's case, there is something utterly new, which changes the world. In the case of our own death, the "going away" is definitive, there is no return. Jesus, on the other hand, says of his death: "I go away, and I will come to you." It is by going away that he comes. His going ushers in a completely new and greater way of being present. By dying he enters into the love of the Father. His dying is an act of love. Love, however, is immortal. Therefore, his going away is transformed into a new coming, into a form of presence which reaches deeper and does not come to an end. During his earthly life, Jesus, like all of us, was

127

tied to the external conditions of bodily existence: to a determined place and a determined time. Bodiliness places limits on our existence. We cannot be simultaneously in two different places. Our time is destined to come to an end. And between the "I" and the "you" there is a wall of otherness. To be sure, through love we can somehow enter the other's existence. Nevertheless, the insurmountable barrier of being different remains in place. Yet Jesus, who is now totally transformed through the act of love, is free from such barriers and limits. He is able not only to pass through closed doors in the outside world, as the Gospels recount (cf. Jn 20:19). He can pass through the interior door separating the "I" from the "you", the closed door between yesterday and today, between the past and the future. On the day of his solemn entry into Jerusalem, when some Greeks asked to see him, Jesus replied with the parable of the grain of wheat which has to pass through death in order to bear much fruit. In this way he foretold his own destiny: these words were not addressed simply to one or two Greeks in the space of a few minutes. Through his Cross, through his going away, through his dying like the grain of wheat, he would truly arrive among the Greeks, in such a way that they could see him and touch him through faith. His going away is transformed into a coming, in the Risen Lord's universal manner of presence, yesterday, today and for ever. He also comes today, and he embraces all times and all places. Now he can even surmount the wall of otherness that separates the "I" from the "you". This happened with Paul, who describes the process of his conversion and his Baptism in these words: "it is no longer I who live, but Christ who lives in me" (Gal 2:20). Through the coming of the Risen One, Paul obtained a new identity. His closed "I" was opened. Now he lives in communion with Jesus Christ, in the great "I" of believers who have become – as he puts it – "one in Christ" (Gal 3:28).

So, it is clear that, through Baptism, the mysterious words spoken by Jesus at the Last Supper become present for you once more. In Baptism, the Lord enters your life through the door of your heart. We no longer stand alongside or in opposition to one another. He passes through all these doors. This is the reality of Baptism: he, the Risen One, comes; he comes to you and joins his life with yours, drawing you into the open fire of his love. You become one, one with him, and thus one among yourselves. At first this can sound rather abstract and unrealistic. But the more you live the life of the baptized, the more you can experience the truth of these words. Believers – the baptized – are never truly cut off from one another. Continents, cultures, social structures or even historical distances may separate us. But when we meet, we know one another on the basis of the same Lord, the same faith, the same hope, the same love, which form us. Then we experience that the foundation of our lives is the same. We experience that in our inmost depths we are anchored in the same identity, on the basis of which all our outward differences, however great they may be, become secondary. Believers are never totally cut off from one another. We are in communion because of our deepest identity: Christ within us. Thus faith is a force for peace and reconciliation in the world: distances between people are overcome, in the Lord we have become close (cf. Eph 2:13).

The Church expresses the inner reality of Baptism as the gift of a new identity through the tangible elements used in the administration of the sacrament. The fundamental element in Baptism is water; next, in second place, is light, which is used to great effect in the Liturgy of the Easter Vigil. Let us take a brief look at these two elements. In the final chapter of the Letter to the Hebrews, there is a statement about Christ which does not speak directly of water, but the Old Testament allusions nevertheless point clearly to the mystery of water and its symbolic meaning. Here we read: "The God of peace ... brought again from the dead our Lord Jesus, the great shepherd of the sheep, by the blood of the eternal covenant" (13:20). In this sentence, there is an echo of the prophecy of Isaiah, in which Moses is described as the shepherd whom the Lord brought up from the water, from the sea (cf. 63:11). And Jesus now appears as the new, definitive Shepherd who brings to fulfillment what Moses had done: he leads us out of the deadly waters of the sea, out of the waters of death. In this context we may recall that Moses' mother placed him in a basket in the

Nile. Then, through God's providence, he was taken out of the water, carried from death to life, and thus – having himself been saved from the waters of death – he was able to lead others through the sea of death. Jesus descended for us into the dark waters of death. But through his blood, so the Letter to the Hebrews tells us, he was brought back from death: his love united itself to the Father's love, and thus from the abyss of death he was able to rise to life. Now he raises us from the waters of death to true life. This is exactly what happens in Baptism: he draws us towards himself, he draws us into true life. He leads us through the often murky sea of history, where we are frequently in danger of sinking amid all the confusion and perils. In Baptism he takes us, as it were, by the hand, he leads us along the path that passes through the Red Sea of this life and introduces us to everlasting life, the true and upright life. Let us grasp his hand firmly! Whatever may happen, whatever may befall us, let us not lose hold of his hand! Let us walk along the path that leads to life.

In the second place, there is the symbol of light and fire. Gregory of Tours (4th century) recounts a practice that in some places was preserved for a long time, of lighting the new fire for the celebration of the Easter Vigil directly from the sun, using a crystal.Light and fire, so to speak, were received anew from heaven, so that all the lights and fires of the year could be kindled from them. This is a symbol of what we are celebrating in the Easter Vigil. Through his radical love for us, in which the heart of God and the heart of man touched, Jesus Christ truly took light from heaven and brought it to the earth – the light of truth and the fire of love that transform man's being. He brought the light, and now we know who God is and what God is like. Thus we also know what our human situation is: what we are, and for what purpose we exist. When we are baptized, the fire of this light is brought down deep within ourselves. Thus, in the early Church, Baptism was also called the Sacrament of Illumination: God's light enters into us; thus we ourselves become children of light. We must not allow this light of truth, that shows us the path, to be extinguished. We must protect it from all the forces that seek to eliminate it so as to cast us back into darkness regarding God and ourselves. Darkness, at times, can seem comfortable. I can hide, and spend my life asleep. Yet we are not called to darkness, but to light. In our baptismal promises, we rekindle this light, so to speak, year by year. Yes, I believe that the world and my life are not the product of chance, but of eternal Reason and eternal Love, they are created by Almighty God. Yes, I believe that in Jesus Christ, in his incarnation, in his Cross and resurrection, the face of God has been revealed; that in him, God is present in our midst, he unites us and leads us towards our goal, towards eternal Love. Yes, I believe that the Holy Spirit gives us the word of truth and enlightens our hearts; I believe that in the communion of the Church we all become one Body with the Lord, and thus we encounter his resurrection and eternal life. The Lord has granted us the light of truth. This light is also fire, a powerful force coming from God, a force that does not destroy, but seeks to transform our hearts, so that we truly become men of God, and so that his peace can become active in this world.

In the early Church there was a custom whereby the Bishop or the priest, after the homily, would cry out to the faithful: "*Conversi ad Dominum*" – turn now towards the Lord. This meant in the first place that they would turn towards the East, towards the rising sun, the sign of Christ returning, whom we go to meet when we celebrate the Eucharist. Where this was not possible, for some reason, they would at least turn towards the image of Christ in the apse, or towards the Cross, so as to orient themselves inwardly towards the Lord. Fundamentally, this involved an interior event; *conversion*, the turning of our soul towards Jesus Christ and thus towards the living God, towards the true light. Linked with this, then, was the other exclamation that still today, before the Eucharistic Prayer, is addressed to the community of the faithful: "*Sursum corda*" – "Lift up your hearts", high above all our misguided concerns, desires, anxieties and thoughtlessness – "Lift up your hearts, your inner selves!" In both exclamations we are summoned, as it were, to a renewal of our Baptism: *Conversi ad Dominum* – we must always turn away from false paths, onto which we stray so often in our thoughts and actions. We must turn ever anew towards him who is the Way, the Truth and the Life. We must be converted ever anew, turning with our whole life towards the Lord. And ever anew we must withdraw our hearts from the force of gravity, which pulls them down, and inwardly we must raise them high: in truth and love. At this hour, let us thank the Lord, because through the power of his word and of the holy Sacraments, he points us in the right direction and draws our heart upwards. Let us pray to him in these words: Yes, Lord, make us Easter people, men and women of light, filled with the fire of your love.

The bread of life

On the eve of his Passion, during the Passover meal, the Lord took the bread in his hands – as we heard a short time ago in the Gospel passage – and, having blessed it, he broke it and gave it to his Disciples, saying: "Take this, this is my body". He then took the chalice, gave thanks and passed it to them and they all drank from it. He said: "This is my blood, the blood of the covenant, to be poured out on behalf of many" (Mk 14:22-24).

The entire history of God with humanity is recapitulated in these words. The past alone is not only referred to and interpreted, but the future is anticipated – the coming of the Kingdom of God into the world. What Jesus says are not simply words. What he says is an event, the central event of the history of the world and of our personal lives.

These words are inexhaustible. In this hour, I would like to meditate with you on just one aspect. Jesus, as a sign of his presence, chose bread and wine. With each one of the two signs he gives himself completely, not only in part. The Risen One is not divided. He is a person who, through signs, comes near to us and unites himself to us. Each sign however, represents in its own way a particular aspect of his mystery and through its respective manifestation, wishes to speak to us so that we learn to understand the mystery of Jesus Christ a little better. During the procession and in adoration we look at the consecrated Host, the most simple type of bread and nourishment, made only of a little flour and water. In this way, it appears as the food of the poor, those to whom the Lord made himself closest in the first place. The prayer with which the Church, during the liturgy of the Mass, consigns this bread to the Lord, qualifies it as fruit of the earth and the work of humans. It involves human labour, the daily work of those who till the soil, sow and harvest [the wheat] and, finally, prepare the bread. However, bread is not purely and simply what we produce, something made by us; it is fruit of the earth and therefore is also gift. We cannot take credit for the fact that the earth produces fruit; the Creator alone could have made it fertile. And now we too can expand a little on this prayer of the Church, saying: the bread is fruit of heaven and earth together. It implies the synergy of the forces of earth and the gifts from above, that is, of the sun and the rain. And water too, which we need to prepare the bread, cannot be produced by us. In a period in which desertification is spoken of and where we hear time and again the warning that man and beast risk dying of thirst in these waterless regions – in such a period we realize once again how great is the gift of water and of how we are unable to produce it ourselves. And so, looking closely at this little piece of white Host, this bread of the poor, appears to us as a synthesis of creation. Heaven and earth, too, like the activity and spirit of man, cooperate. The synergy of the forces that make the mystery of life and the existence of man possible on our poor planet come to meet us in all of their majestic grandeur. In this way we begin to understand why the Lord chooses this piece of bread to represent him. Creation, with all of its gifts, aspires above and beyond itself to something even greater. Over and above the synthesis of its own forces, above and beyond the synthesis also of nature and of spirit that, in some way, we detect in the piece of bread, creation is projected towards divinization, toward the holy wedding feast, toward unification with the Creator himself.

And still, we have not yet explained in depth the message of this sign of bread. The Lord mentioned its deepest mystery on Palm Sunday, when some Greeks asked to see him. In his answer to this question is the phrase: "Truly, truly, I say to you, unless a grain of wheat falls into the earth and dies, it remains alone; but if it dies, it bears much fruit" (Jn 12:24). The mystery of the Passion is hidden in the bread made of ground grain. Flour, the ground wheat, presuppose the death and resurrection of the grain. In being ground and baked, it carries in itself once again the same mystery of the Passion. Only through death does resurrection arrive, as does the fruit and new life. Mediterranean culture, in the centuries before Christ, had a profound intuition of this mystery. Based on the experience of this death and rising they created myths of divinity which, dying and rising, gave new life. To them, the cycle of nature seemed like a divine promise in the midst of the darkness of suffering and death that we are faced with. In these myths, the soul of the human person, in a certain way, reached out toward that God made man, who, humiliated unto death on a cross, in this way opened the door of life to all of us. In bread and its making, man has understood it as a waiting period of nature, like a promise of nature that this would come to exist: the God that dies and in this way brings us to life. What was awaited in myths and that in the very grain of wheat is hidden like a sign of the hope of creation – this truly came about in Christ. Through his gratuitous suffering and death, he became bread for all of us, and with this living and certain hope. He accompanies us in all of our sufferings until death. The paths that he travels with us and through which he leads us to life are pathways of hope.

When, in adoration, we look at the consecrated Host, the sign of creation speaks to us. And so, we encounter the greatness of his gift; but we also encounter the Passion, the Cross of Jesus and his Resurrection. Through this gaze of adoration, he draws us toward himself, within his mystery, through which he wants to transform us as he transformed the Host.

The mercy of God is greater than our guilt

Lent is an especially favourable season to meditate on the reality of sin in the light of God's infinite mercy, which the Sacrament of Penance expresses in its loftiest form. I therefore willingly take this opportunity to bring to your attention certain thoughts on the administration of this Sacrament in our time, in which the loss of the sense of sin is unfortunately becoming increasingly more widespread. It is necessary today to assist those who confess to experience that divine tenderness to repentant sinners which many Gospel episodes portray with tones of deep feeling. Let us take, for example, the passage in Luke's Gospel that presents the woman who was a sinner and was forgiven (cf. Lk 7:36-50). Simon, a Pharisee and a rich dignitary of the town, was holding a banquet at his home in honour of Jesus. In accordance with a custom of that time, the meal was eaten with the doors left open, for in this way the fame and prestige of the homeowner was increased. All at once, an uninvited and unexpected guest entered from the back of the room: a well-known prostitute. One can understand the embarrassment of those present, which did not seem, however, to bother the woman. She came forward and somewhat furtively stopped at Jesus' feet. She had heard his words of pardon and hope for all, even prostitutes; she was moved and stayed where she was in silence. She bathed Jesus' feet with tears, wiped them dry with her hair, kissed them and anointed them with fragrant ointment. By so doing, the sinner woman wanted to express her love for and gratitude to the Lord with gestures that were familiar to her, although they were censured by society.

Amid the general embarrassment, it was Jesus himself who saved the situation: "Simon, I have something to say to you". "What is it, Teacher?", the master of the house asked him. We all know Jesus' answer with a parable which we can sum up in the following words which the Lord addressed basically to Simon: "You see? This woman knows she is a sinner; yet prompted by love, she is asking for understanding and forgiveness. You, on the other hand, presume yourself to be righteous and are perhaps convinced that you have nothing serious for which to be forgiven".

The message that shines out from this Gospel passage is eloquent: God forgives all to those who love much. Those who trust in themselves and in their own merits are, as it were, blinded by their ego and their heart is hardened in sin. Those, on the other hand, who recognize that they are weak and sinful entrust themselves to God and obtain from him grace and forgiveness. It is precisely this message that must be transmitted: what counts most is to make people understand that in the Sacrament of Reconciliation, whatever the sin committed, if it is humbly recognized and the person involved turns with trust to the priest-confessor, he or she never fails to experience the soothing joy of God's forgiveness. In this perspective your Course acquires considerable importance. It aims to prepare well-trained confessors from the doctrinal viewpoint who are able to make their penitents experience the Heavenly Father's merciful love. Might it not be true that today we are witnessing a certain alienation from this Sacrament? When one insists solely on the accusation of sins – which must nevertheless exist and it is necessary to help the faithful understand its importance – one risks relegating to the background what is central, that is, the personal encounter with God, the Father of goodness and mercy. It is not sin which is at the heart of the sacramental celebration but rather God's mercy, which is infinitely greater than any guilt of ours.

It must be a commitment of pastors and especially of confessors to highlight the close connection that exists between the Sacrament of Reconciliation and a life oriented decisively to conversion. It is necessary that between the practice of the Sacrament of Confession and a life in which a person strives to follow Christ sincerely, a sort of continuous "virtuous circle" be established in which the grace of the Sacrament may sustain and nourish the commitment to be a faithful disciple of the Lord. The Lenten Season, in which we now find ourselves, reminds us that in our Christian life we must always aspire to conversion and that when we receive the Sacrament of Reconciliation frequently the desire for Gospel perfection is kept alive in believers. If this constant desire is absent, the celebration of the Sacrament unfortunately risks becoming something formal that has no effect on the fabric of daily life. If, moreover, even when one is motivated by the desire to follow Jesus one does not go regularly to confession, one risks gradually slowing his or her spiritual pace to the point of increasingly weakening and ultimately perhaps even exhausting it.

Dear brothers, it is not difficult to understand the value in the Church of your ministry as stewards of divine mercy for the salvation of souls. Persevere in imitating the example of so many holy confessors who, with their spiritual insight, helped penitents to understand that the regular celebration of the Sacrament of Penance and a Christian life that aspires to holiness are inseparable elements of the same spiritual process for every baptized person. And do not forget that you yourselves are examples of authentic Christian life. May the Virgin Mary, Mother of Mercy and of Hope, help you who are present here and all confessors to carry out zealously and joyfully this great service on which the Church's life so intensely depends.

The viaticum of the sick

Jesus did not only send his disciples forth to heal the sick (cf. Mt 10:8; Lk 9:2, 10:9); he also instituted a specific sacrament for them: the Anointing of the Sick. The Letter of James attests to the presence of this sacramental sign in the early Christian community (cf. 5:14-16). If the Eucharist shows how Christ's sufferings and death have been transformed into love, the Anointing of the Sick, for its part, unites the sick with Christ's self-offering for the salvation of all, so that they too, within the mystery of the communion of saints, can participate in the redemption of the world. The relationship between these two sacraments becomes clear in situations of serious illness: "In addition to the Anointing of the Sick, the Church offers those who are about to leave this life the Eucharist as viaticum." (67) On their journey to the Father, communion in the Body and Blood of Christ appears as the seed of eternal life and the power of resurrection: "Anyone who eats my flesh and drinks my blood has eternal life and I will raise him up on the last day" (Jn 6:54). Since viaticum gives the sick a glimpse of the fullness of the Paschal Mystery, its administration should be readily provided for. (68) Attentive pastoral care shown to those who are ill brings great spiritual benefit to the entire community, since whatever we do to one of the least of our brothers and sisters, we do to Jesus himself (cf. Mt 25:40).

ETERNAL LIFE

The belief in eternal life

We must ask explicitly: is the Christian faith also for us today a life-changing and life-sustaining hope?

Is it "performative" for us – is it a message which shapes our life in a new way, or is it just "information" which, in the meantime, we have set aside and which now seems to us to have been superseded by more recent information? In the search for an answer, I would like to begin with the classical form of the dialogue with which the rite of Baptism expressed the reception of an infant into the community of believers and the infant's rebirth in Christ. First of all the priest asked what name the parents had chosen for the child, and then he continued with the question: "What do you ask of the Church?" Answer: "Faith". "And what does faith give you?" "Eternal life". According to this dialogue, the parents were seeking access to the faith for their child, communion with believers, because they saw in faith the key to "eternal life". Today as in the past, this is what being baptized, becoming Christians, is all about: it is not just an act of socialization within the community, not simply a welcome into the Church. The parents expect more for the one to be baptized: they expect that faith, which includes the corporeal nature of the Church and her sacraments, will give life to their child – eternal life. Faith is the substance of hope. But then the question arises: do we really want this – to live eternally? Perhaps many people reject the faith today simply because they do not find the prospect of eternal life attractive. What they desire is not eternal life at all, but this present life, for which faith in eternal life seems something of an impediment. To continue living for ever – endlessly – appears more like a curse than a gift. Death, admittedly, one would wish to postpone for as long as possible. But to live always, without end – this, all things considered, can only be monotonous and ultimately unbearable. This is precisely the point made, for example, by Saint Ambrose, one of the Church Fathers, in the funeral discourse for his deceased brother Satyrus: "Death was not part of nature; it became part of nature. God did not decree death from the beginning; he prescribed it as a remedy. Human life, because of sin ... began to experience the burden of wretchedness in unremitting labour and unbearable sorrow. There had to be a limit to its evils; death had to restore what life had forfeited. Without the assistance of grace, immortality is more of a burden than a blessing"[1]. A little earlier, Ambrose had said: "Death is, then, no cause for mourning, for it is the cause of mankind's salvation"[2].

Whatever precisely Saint Ambrose may have meant by these words, it is true that to eliminate death or to postpone it more or less indefinitely would place the earth and humanity in an impossible situation, and even for the individual would bring no benefit. Obviously there is a contradiction in our attitude, which points to an inner contradiction in our very existence. On the one hand, we do not want to die; above all, those who love us do not want us to die. Yet on the other hand, neither do we want to continue living indefinitely, nor was the earth created with that in view. So what do we really want? Our paradoxical attitude gives rise to a deeper question: what in fact is "life"? And what does "eternity" really mean? There are moments when it suddenly seems clear to us: yes, this is what true "life" is – this is what it should be like. Besides, what we call "life" in our everyday language is not real "life" at all. Saint Augustine, in the extended letter on prayer which he addressed to Proba, a wealthy Roman widow and mother of three consuls, once wrote this: ultimately we want only one thing – "the blessed life", the life which is simply life, simply "happiness". In the final analysis, there is nothing else that we ask for in prayer. Our journey has no other goal – it is about this alone. But then Augustine also says: looking more closely, we have no idea what we ultimately desire, what we would really like. We do not know this reality at all; even in those moments when we think we can reach out and touch it, it eludes us. "We do not know what we should pray for as we ought," he says, quoting Saint Paul (Rom 8:26). All we know is that it is not this. Yet in not knowing, we know that this reality must exist. "There is therefore in us a certain learned ignorance (*docta ignorantia*), so to speak", he writes. We do not know what we would really like; we do not know this "true life"; and yet we know that there must be something we do not know towards which we feel driven[3].

I think that in this very precise and permanently valid way, Augustine is describing man's essential situation, the situation that gives rise to all his contradictions and hopes. In some way we want life itself, true life, untouched even by death; yet at the same time we do not know the thing towards which we feel driven. We cannot stop reaching out for it, and yet we know that all we can experience or accomplish is not what we yearn for. This unknown "thing" is the true "hope" which drives us, and at the same time the fact that it is unknown is the cause of all forms of despair and also of all efforts, whether positive or destructive, directed towards worldly authenticity and human authenticity. The term "eternal life" is intended to give a name to this known "unknown". Inevitably it is an inadequate term that creates confusion. "Eternal", in fact, suggests to us the idea of something interminable, and this frightens us; "life" makes us think of the life that we know and love and do not want to lose, even though very often it brings more toil than satisfaction, so that while on the one hand we desire it, on the other hand we do not want it. To imagine ourselves outside the temporality that imprisons us and in some way to sense that eternity is not an unending succession of days in the calendar, but something more like the supreme moment of satisfaction, in which totality embraces us and we embrace totality – this we can only attempt. It would be like plunging into the ocean of infinite love, a moment in which time – the before and after – no longer exists. We can only attempt to grasp the idea that such a moment is life in the full sense, a plunging ever anew into the vastness of being, in which we are simply overwhelmed with joy. This is how Jesus expresses it in Saint John's Gospel: "I will see you again and your hearts will rejoice, and no one will take your joy from you" (16:22). We must think along these lines if we want to understand the object of Christian hope, to understand what it is that our faith, our being with Christ, leads us to expect.

An irrepressible longing

The feast of All Saints brought us to contemplate "your holy city, the heavenly Jerusalem, our mother" (*Preface, All Saints*). Today, with our heart still turned toward this ultimate reality, we commemorate all of the faithful departed, who have "gone before us marked with the sign of faith and... who sleep in Christ" (*Eucharistic Prayer I*).

It is very important that we Christians live a relationship of the truth of the faith with the deceased and that we view death and the afterlife in the light of Revelation. Already the Apostle Paul, writing to the first communities, exhorted the faithful to "not grieve as others do who have no hope. For since", he wrote, "we believe that Jesus died and rose again, even so, through Jesus, God will bring with him those who have fallen asleep" (1 Thes 4:13-14). Today too, it is necessary to evangelize about the reality of death and eternal life, realities particularly subject to superstitious beliefs and syncretisms, so that the Christian truth does not risk mixing itself with myths of various types.

In my Encyclical on Christian hope, I questioned myself about the mystery of eternal life (cf. *Spe salvi*, 10-12). I asked myself: "Is the Christian faith a hope that transforms and sustains the lives of people still today?" (cf. *ibid.*, n. 10). And more radically: "Do men and women of our time still long for eternal life? Or has earthly existence perhaps become their only horizon?" In reality, as St Augustine had already observed, all of us want a "blessed life", happiness. We rarely know what it is like or how it will be, but we feel attracted to it. This is a universal hope, common to men and women of all times and all places. The expression "eternal life" aims to give a name to this irrepressible longing; it is not an unending succession of days, but an immersion of oneself in the ocean of infinite love, in which time, before and after, no longer exists. A fullness of life and of joy: it is this that we hope and await from our being with Christ (cf. *ibid*, 12).

Today we renew the hope in eternal life, truly founded on Christ's death and Resurrection. "I am risen and I am with you always", the Lord tells us, and my hand supports you. Wherever you may fall, you will fall into my hands and I will be there even to the gates of death. Where no one can accompany you any longer and where you can take nothing with you, there I will wait for you to transform for you the darkness into light. Christian hope, however, is not solely individual, it is also always a hope for others. Our lives are profoundly linked, one to the other, and the good and the bad that each of us does always effects others too. Hence, the prayer of a pilgrim soul in the world can help another soul that is being purified after death. This is why the Church invites us today to pray for our beloved deceased and to pause at their tombs in the cemeteries. Mary, Star of Hope, renders our faith in eternal life stronger and more authentic, and supports our prayer of suffrage for our deceased brethren.

Whoever believes in me will live

I would like to offer a few simple thoughts on the reality of death, which for us Christians is illuminated by the Resurrection of Christ, and so as to renew our faith in eternal life.

We go to the cemetery to pray for the loved ones who have left us, as it were paying a visit to show them, once more, our love, to feel them still close, remembering also, an article of the Creed: in the communion of saints there is a close bond between us who are still walking here upon the earth and those many brothers and sisters who have already entered eternity.

Human beings have always cared for their dead and sought to give them a sort of second life through attention, care and affection. In a way, we want to preserve their experience of life; and, paradoxically, by looking at their graves, before which countless memories return, we discover how they lived, what they loved, what they feared, what they hoped for and what they hated. They are almost a mirror of their world.

Why is this so? Because, despite the fact that death is an almost forbidden subject in our society and that there is a continuous attempt to banish the thought of it from our minds, death touches each of us, it touches mankind of every age and every place. And before this mystery we all, even unconsciously, search for something to give us hope, a sign that might bring us consolation, open up some horizon, offer us a future once more. The road to death, in reality, is a way of hope and it passes through our cemeteries, just as can be read on the tombstones and fulfills a journey marked by the hope of eternity.

Yet, we wonder, why do we feel fear before death? Why has humanity, for the most part, never resigned itself to the belief that beyond life there is simply nothing? I would say that there are multiple answers: we are afraid of death because we are afraid of that nothingness, of leaving this world for something we don't know, something unknown to us. And, then, there is a sense of rejection in us because we cannot accept that all that is beautiful and great, realized during a lifetime, should be suddenly erased, should fall into the abyss of nothingness. Above all, we feel that love calls and asks for eternity and it is impossible to accept that it is destroyed by death in an instant.

Furthermore, we fear in the face of death because, when we find ourselves approaching the end of our lives, there is a perception that our actions will be judged, the way in which we have lived our lives, above all, those moments of darkness which we often skillfully remove or try to remove from our conscience. I would say that precisely the question of judgment often underlies man of all time's concern for the dead, the attention paid to the people who were important to him and are no longer with him on the journey through earthly life. In a certain sense the gestures of affection and love which surround the deceased are a way to protect him in the conviction that they will have an effect on the judgment. This we can gather from the majority of cultures that characterize the history of man.

Today the world has become, at least in appearance, much more rational, or rather, there is a more widespread tendency to think that every reality ought to be tackled with the criteria of experimental science, and that the great questions about death ought to be answered not so much with faith as with empirical, provable knowledge. It is not sufficiently taken into account, however, that precisely in this way one is doomed to fall into forms of spiritism, in an attempt to have some kind of contact with the world beyond, almost imagining it to be a reality that, ultimately, is a copy of the present one.

The Solemnity of All Saints and the Commemoration of all the faithful departed tells us that only those who can recognize a great hope in death, can live a life based on hope. If we reduce man exclusively to his horizontal dimension, to that which can be perceived empirically, life itself loses its profound meaning. Man needs eternity for every other hope is too brief, too limited for him. Man can be explained only if there is a Love which overcomes every isolation, even that of death, in a totality which also transcends time and space. Man can be explained, he finds his deepest meaning, only if there is God. And we know that God left his distance for us and made himself close. He entered into our life and tells us: "I am the resurrection and the life; he who believes in me, though he die, yet shall he live, and whoever lives and believes in me shall never die" (Jn 11:25-26).

Let us think for a moment of the scene on Calvary and listen again to Jesus' words from the height of the Cross, addressed to the criminal crucified on his right: "Truly, I say to you, today you will be with me in Paradise" (Lk 23:43). We think of the two disciples on the road to Emmaus, when, after travelling a stretch of the way with the Risen Jesus, they recognize him and set out immediately for Jerusalem to proclaim the Resurrection of the Lord (cf. Lk 24:13-35). The Master's words come back to our minds with renewed clarity: "Let not your hearts be troubled; believe in God, believe also in me. In my Father's house are many rooms; if it were not so, would I have told you that I go to prepare a place for you?" (Jn 14:1-2). God is truly demonstrated, he became accessible, for he so loved the world "that he gave his only Son, that whoever believes in him should not perish but have eternal life" (Jn 3:16), and in the supreme act of love on the Cross, immersing himself in the abyss of death, he conquered it, and rose and opened the doors of eternity for us too. Christ sustains us through the night of death which he himself overcame; he is the Good Shepherd, on whose guidance one can rely without any fear, for he knows the way well, even through darkness.

Every Sunday in reciting the Creed, we reaffirm this truth. And in going to cemeteries to pray with affection and love for our departed, we are invited, once more, to renew with courage and with strength our faith in eternal life, indeed to live with this great hope and to bear witness to it in the world: behind the present there is not nothing. And faith in eternal life gives to Christians the courage to love our earth ever more intensely and to work in order to build a future for it, to give it a true and sure hope.

The end of our journey

St Peter, in the Acts of the Apostles, says that God exalted Jesus at his right hand as Leader and Saviour (cf. Acts 5: 31). Leader is a translation of the Greek terms *archēgos,*

153

which implies a far more dynamic vision: *archēgos* is the one who shows the way, who goes ahead, it is a movement, an upwards movement. God raised him at his right hand therefore, speaking of Christ as *archēgos* means that Christ walks before us, he precedes us, he shows us the way. And being in communion with Christ is being on the way, it is climbing with Christ, it is following Christ, it is the ascent, it is following the *archēgos,* the One who has gone before, who precedes us and points out the way.

Here, evidently, it is important that we are told where Christ arrives and where we too must arrive: *hypsōsen* on high ascending to the right hand of the Father. The "sequela" of Christ is not only the imitation of his virtues, it is not only living in this world, as far we are able, as Christ lived, in accordance with his words, but it is a journey that has a destination. And the destination is the right hand of the Father. There is this journey of Jesus, this following of Jesus which ends at the right hand of the Father. The whole of Jesus' journey, even reaching the right hand of the Father fits into the horizon of this "sequela".

In this regard the destination of this journey is eternal life at the right hand of the Father in communion with Christ. Today all too often we are somewhat afraid of speaking about eternal life. We talk of things that are useful for the world, we show that Christianity also helps us to improve the world, but we do not dare to say that its destination is eternal life and that from this destination stem the criteria for life. We must understand anew that Christianity remains a "fragment" unless we think of this destination, that we want to follow the *archegos* to God's height, to the glory of the Son who makes us sons in the Son, and we must once again recognize that only in the great perspective of eternal life does Christianity reveal its full meaning. We must have the courage, the joy, the great hope that eternal life exists, it is the true life and from this true life comes the light that also illuminates this world.

One may even say leaving aside eternal life, the Heaven promised that it is better to live in accordance with Christian criteria because living in accordance with truth and love, even in the midst of so much persecution is in itself good and is better than everything else. It is precisely this will to live in accordance with truth and love that must also be open to the whole breadth of God's plan with us, to the courage to jubilate already at the prospect of eternal life, the ascent, following our *archēgos*. And *Sōtēr* is the Saviour, who saves us from ignorance, in seeking the last things. The Saviour saves us from solitude; he saves us from the emptiness that pervades life without eternity; he saves us by giving us love in its fullness. He is the guide. Christ, the *archēgos*, saves us by giving us the light, giving us the truth, giving us the love of God.

Next let us reflect further on this verse: Christ, the Saviour, gave to Israel repentance and forgiveness of sins (v.31) in the Greek text the term is *metanoia* he gave repentance and pardon for sins. This to me is a very important observation: repentance is a grace. There is an exegetical trend that states that in Galilee Jesus would have proclaimed a grace without conditions, absolutely

155

unconditional, therefore also without penitence, grace as such, without human preconditions. But this is a false interpretation of grace. Repentance is grace; it is a grace that we recognize our sin; it is a grace that we realize the need for renewal, for change, for the transformation of our being. Repentance the capacity to be penitent, is a gift of grace. And I must say that we Christians, even in recent times, have often avoided the word penitence, it seemed to us too difficult. Now, under the attacks of the world that speak of our sins, we see that the capacity to repent is a grace. And we see that it is necessary to do penance, that is, to recognize what is wrong in our lives, open ourselves to forgiveness, prepare ourselves for pardon by allowing ourselves to be transformed.

The pain of repentance, of purification and of transformation this pain is a grace, because it is renewal, it is a work of divine mercy. And thus these two things of which St Peter speaks – repentance and forgiveness – correspond to Jesus' initial preaching: *metanoeite*, in other words, "repent" (cf. Mk 1:15). Therefore this is the fundamental point: *metanoia* is not a private affair, which appears to be substituted by grace, but rather *metanoia* is the advent of grace that transforms us. And in conclusion, one word of the Gospel, in which we are told that whoever believes will have eternal life (cf. Jn 3:36). In faith, in this "transformation" that repentance brings, in this conversion, in this new way of living, we arrive at life, at real life. At this point two other texts come to mind. In the "priestly prayer" the Lord says: this is life, knowing you and your Anointed. (cf. Jn 17:3). Understanding the essential, knowing the decisive Person, knowing God and the One whom he has sent is life, life and understanding, the understanding of the realities that constitute life. And the other text is the response of the Lord to the Sadducees regarding the Resurrection, when, using the Books of Moses, the Lord proves the Resurrection as a fact, by saying: God is the God of Abraham, of Isaac, of Jacob (cf. Mt 22:31-32; Mk 12:26-27; Lk 20:37-38). God is not a God of the dead. If God is the God of these, then they live. Whoever is inscribed in God's name participates in God's life, and lives. Therefore to believe is to be inscribed in the name of God. Thus we are alive. Whoever has a share in God's name is not dead but rather belongs to the living God. In this sense we should be able to understand the dynamism of faith, which entails enrolling our names in the name of God and in this way entering into life.

ENDNOTES

1. *De excessu fratris sui Satyri*, II, 47: *CSEL* 73, 274.
2. *Ibid.*, II, 46: *CSEL* 73, 273.
3. Cf. Ep. 130 *Ad Probam* 14, 25-15, 28: *CSEL* 44, 68-73.

SOURCES

The source of all truth: Address, Ecumenical Prayer Service, Church of the former Augustinian Convent, Erfurt, Friday, 23 September 2011

One God, Deus caritas est, n. 9.

Creator of heaven and earth: Homily, St Peter's Basilica, 23 April 2011

The language of creation: Caritas in veritate, n. 48.

The great hope: Spe salvi, n. 27.

The two dimensions of love: Deus caritas est, nn. 16-18.

The revelation of God's love: Message for Lent 2007

King of the poor and king of peace: Homily, St Peter's Square, Palm Sunday, 9 April 2006

He suffered under Pontius Pilate: General Audience, St Peter's Square, Wednesday, 8 April 2009

He was crucified, died and was buried: General Audience, St Peter's Square, Wednesday, 8 April 2009

On the third day he rose again: General Audience, St Peter's Square, Wednesday, 5 November 2008

He ascended into heaven and is seated at the right hand of the Father: Homily, Bentegodi Stadium, Thursday, 19 October 2006

His kingdom will have no end: Homily, Vatican Basilica, Solemnity of Christ the King of the Universe, Sunday, 21 November 2010

The Spirit of God: Homily, St Peter's Square, Saturday, 3 June 2006

The Lord, the giver of life: Address to the Members of the Roman Curia, Clementine Hall, Monday, 22 December 2008

He has spoken through the Prophets: Address to the Members of the Roman Curia, Clementine Hall, Monday, 22 December 2008

Come, Holy Spirit: Homily, St Peter's Basilica, Sunday, 23 May 2010

The Holy Spirit in the life of the Church: General Audience, Wednesday, 26 April 2006

The breath of christian life: Message to the Young People of the World on the Occasion of the XXIII World Youth Day, 2008